AWESOMISM!

✦

A New Way to Understand the Diagnosis of Autism

Suzy Miller

iUniverse, Inc.
New York   Bloomington

AWESOMISM!

A New Way to Understand the Diagnosis of Autism

iUniverse books may be ordered through booksellers or by contacting:

iUniverse
1663 Liberty Drive
Bloomington, IN 47403
www.iuniverse.com
1-800-Authors (1-800-288-4677)

ISBN: 978-1-4401-0285-1 (pbk)
ISBN: 978-1-4401-0286-8 (ebk)

Printed in the United States of America

"A person's a person, no matter how small."
Dr. Seuss, *Horton Hears a Who*

Dedication

This book is dedicated to my four beautiful daughters in gratitude for all that they have taught me and for their love which soars beyond the standards of typical mother-daughter relationships. I am truly blessed to have them in my life, specifically to Rachel who taught me about individuality and independence, to Catie for teaching me tenderness and comfort, to Maria for courage and wisdom and to Laura for deep insight mixed with the right dose of humor. I have been blessed in each moment and every relationship to learn and grow by those closest to me and by those who came to provide the support and awareness needed at just the right moment...in just the right manner. A special thank you and blessing to each of the following, who supported me through this journey through the demonstration of their own unique gifts. Annimac for reminding how to be 100% "me to the max" and the strength that is inherent in "walking the talk", to Steve Strange for presence and moving beyond the old to create a new moment, in each moment, to Terry-Damlos Mitchell for laughter, loads of fun and several unexplainable experiences, to Sheila Waugh-Klink for constantly reminding me to go "deeper than that", to Mary Cole for grace of being and the capacity to hold a space for all emotion, to Jennifer Crews for providing an amazing mirror reflection of my process and clear insights, to Jill Turner for her ability to allow me a magnificent playground for the fullest expression of my multidimensional awareness and her ability to be in compassion always, to Ann Hurst for her consistent support and encouragement from my first meeting with Riley until the present moment, to Laura Alden Kamm for her amazingly clear foresight to see this coming long before I could and her gentle nudges along the way, to Gary and Sally Vulcano for being an amazing catalyst into new beginnings, to Gary Kadi for motivation with a capital M and the chance meeting of a life time, to Michael Levin with deep gratitude for turning my experiences, thoughts and words into a manuscript that could be clearly understood and of benefit to all who read it, to my mother and sister for being the roots and foundation from which all experiences grow and last but not least to Riley and all the children that have been gracious enough to share their Awesomsim with me. Thank you!

Foreward

The moment we recognize our outer environment as seemingly separate from ourselves, our curiosity runs wild. We are eager to find the answers to the *how* and *why* of life and we do so in all manner and style. Like the infant who miraculously discovers its toes. The toddler who gets her initial gritty taste of earth. The daring adolescent curious to discover if their warm wet tongue really does adhere to an icy metal pole. Or perhaps the scientist who searches the heavens or watches a laser split atoms. As human beings, we search.

We search for pathways of understanding and resolve. We use our minds and senses to observe and collect information for the purpose of satisfying our inquisitiveness about life and to calm our fears of the unknown. Science, religion and philosophy keep our discoveries and beliefs congruent and neatly accessible for current and future generations. Yet, in light of our attempt to organize our world through systems and calculations, we also recognize that every thought, every systematic lens through which we perceive and navigate our world, at some point in time arrives at a new horizon. A place where that which was once held true and dear is challenged by the ever-changing nature of life. Based on this guarantee of impermanence, perceptions do change yet again.

Quantum science tells us that the consciousness that makes up the "you" and "I" of the world is truly interconnected to all other things. We are not separate at all. We participate, consciously or unconsciously, in a universe that is constructed of a vast field of consciousness, of thought. That as participators in this universe we can, with our thoughts, feelings and beliefs, change our world. We can alter what we are participating in simply by thinking about it; whether we are in the location of the object of our thoughts or not. We participate, across time and space with our mind and the unseen energy our thoughts create.

When you approach a new horizon, it is helpful to believe that something new is possible. That is the catalyst that sends your powerful thoughts to the problem at hand, seeking a solution; perhaps, without you consciously knowing it. And with those thoughts of curiosity, healing, hope and courage, you can change the direction of life by bringing forth this new understanding. That is the seed of change.

There are many discoveries yet to be made. And we use our systems and cosmologies to keep our curiosities alive and goals in sight. However, we often find that science and religion, psychology and spirituality have been positioned in opposite corners as we search for answers; which often promote conflict and challenges within ourselves. It has always been precarious to be a rebel. Nonetheless, it is the rebel who, in the end, often produces the gateway that leads humanity into a broader meaning regarding the *why* and *how* of our life and the universe.

Now, with observant, curious and rebellious thinkers in science a new gateway of perception has been sanctioned. It is a perspective which reflects that which has been held sacred by ancient sages and mystics of all religions throughout time. The organic circle of life with its ever-changing continuum has evolved humanity's consciousness into a notable synergistic shift, bringing to light common ground where there was once a dark and vast schism. This emerging world view, an integral view of science, new biology and the field of consciousness notes an interconnection that has always been present to the seers and knowers.

My work in energy medicine has spanned more than three decades. In that time I have witnessed a more solid merger of science and Spirit.

While I have always held the position that science must never dictate or validate one's spiritual experience, I have profound appreciation for that which quantum science espouses and what I have intuitively seen for decades. It gives theoretical support for energy medicine, the field of holistic medicine and the advancement of human consciousness. It is a merger that, indeed, holds the key to a deeper understanding of our truer nature, health and healing.

In *Awesomism* author Suzy Miller, brings us into this newly bridged world of biology, energy medicine, and spirituality and shows us that Autism, in particular, is perhaps not as concretized as it appears to be. According to some, such as Dr. Bruce Lipton, *The Biology of Belief*, Deepak Chopra, *Quantum Healing*, and in my own work, *Intuitive Wellness*, it is noted scientifically, philosophically and spiritually that there is much more behind the nature of a condition than science had once asserted. If that is true, perhaps we can begin to recreate a new definition of autism and other conditions.

What would this perspective of energy, intuition, and interconnectedness do for the children with autism, their parents and siblings? Would it broaden their perspective, creating healing and hope when there was only frustration and struggle? Suzy sets forth to share and explain this bold new perspective based on her keen observation and genuine ability to be that scientific sage who *sees* and *knows*. Based on her findings, children with autism are able to sense energy more astutely than most of us. They have many challenges some of which are, in their energetic world and state of being, they are unable to articulate all they sensed and know. Imagine what it would be like to not have clear lines between the energy of your body and your favorite chair. What if they are challenged in their ability to energetically discern what's theirs and what's yours or where the grass begins and their body ends? Perhaps they see and feel the waves of invisible energy that shatters through the air as a book falls and hits the floor. In order to fully understand these children, we must take these bold steps and unmoor ourselves from past perspectives, reaching with science and spirituality at our side, toward this new horizon.

If we can take a moment and perchance look through their eyes, we may see the world in a new way. What if, as they enter into a room, an autistic child sees all the squares or circles in the room first? Or that they hyper focus on the emotions that hang in the air from the people who just left; be they sad, happy, angry or confused and innocently take on these emotions, making them their own. Because their emotional and energetic navigational tools are inordinately sensitive, they have much with which to cope and much to teach us. We only need to take the step forward in our perspective and be curious enough to learn. Possibly, they see the world that quantum science tells us exists in and around us that we cannot see or hear. Maybe, their world is truly more reflective of our interconnected reality than we had previously thought or could even contemplate.

In *Awesomism,* Suzy takes our hand and lovingly challenges us to look through a new lens when viewing these precious children. She skillfully encourages us to be more open, to love them right where they are and to learn from them. Perhaps they are here to teach us about the subtleties of this world. How would we ever know if we didn't open our minds and attempt to explore their world through keen observation and the harnessing our own intuitive faculty? They deserve our efforts to meet them where they live. These priceless children are, undoubtedly, in our lives to teach us how to take that richer and more mindful walk through life—a walk with our own soul and theirs.

Laura Alden Kamm – author, *Intuitive Wellness; using your body's inner wisdom to heal,* Atria/Beyond Words

Contents

Intention

This book is an invitation to move beyond the diagnosis of autism to the experience of Awesomism.

Its intention is to bring joy, gratitude, and empowerment to the parents and families of these amazing children by offering a perspective that is worthy of the full scope of your child's experience.

Please journey with me and discover the full potential that is Awesomism.

Chapter 1

Riley's Story

You have a child diagnosed with autism. The traditional approaches haven't been satisfactory for you. Now what?

Sometimes in life we choose to expand our awareness of a subject, as you are doing by reading this book, and sometimes situations occur that expand our awareness unexpectedly, as if by fate. I fall into category number two. I never intended to become a writer or to have such a strong interest in autism. I barely wanted to become a speech-language pathologist. I have worked as one for twenty-two years, and in retrospect it has been a perfect fit. The combination of working with small children and my interest in the power of words kept the field of speech-language pathology interesting to me for several years. I had a well-rounded professional experience working in clinics, hospitals, schools, and in private practice. I worked with literally thousands of children with a variety of "delays" and "disorders," and I almost always ended up adoring each of them. Early on I had a strong sense that there was always something deeper associated with their inability to communicate and that was what brought them to me. There was a "something more" to them, and I loved watching that reveal itself to me as our time together progressed. That was especially true for the

1

children who were nonverbal. I frequently wondered what it is about a connection that is beyond words that makes it so powerful. Those were the children who seemed to move me from the inside out.

My own personal experience as a child taught me that there was so much more to me than the adults in my world could see. And thus in my mind as I grew older, I knew there was much more to every child than most could see. I also knew that children were always communicating regardless of whether or not they were speaking.

It seemed that many of the children that I worked with suffered not only from difficulty with communication skills but also from a feeling of insecurity or a lack of trust. It became obvious to me that it was most important to gain a sense of trust and connection with the child, and the communication just came easier.

It also seemed apparent to me from early on that the best practice was to focus on what the child can do versus what they cannot do. By focusing on the "can dos," the hard-to-do things became much easier for them, and so they progressed well. By building a relationship first, focusing on what they can do rather than what they can't, and letting the steps reveal themselves to me, I was able to reach these children, and their ability to communicate flowed quickly and easily.

My training as a speech-language pathologist gave me a hierarchy of thought, a game plan of where to go and how to get there. Although that professional understanding was helpful, I always had a nagging feeling in the back of my mind that what I was doing with the children was less important than how I was being with them. Maybe it was a combination of both, but the fact was that on the rare occasion where I could not connect with a child, the child made very little progress.

Autism was rare when I started work as a speech pathologist in the late eighties. For the first ten years of my practice, I may have seen only one or two children diagnosed with autism. In the eighties, typically only one child in a family would be diagnosed with autism. Now it is not uncommon to see a family with several children who have been diagnosed with this "condition." In 1986, there was no formal training in autism within my master's program. My lack of concrete information about the topic was later to serve me as one of my greatest assets in truly experiencing the full scope of autism, but in the beginning all I could see were the outward behaviors and how they were impeding my client's ability to learn. I saw the running and the screaming, the tantrums and the ritualistic behavior. I saw downright defiance at worst and a general lack of participation at best. I had to let my first client diagnosed with autism go. As a speech-language pathologist, I didn't think there was anything that I could do for her. My way of connecting to my other children did not work with her. I had such a hard time seeing beyond everything that seemed to be getting in the way of her progress. The behaviors seemed to be front and center all the time, which made it very difficult to see anything else. Thank goodness that limited perception was not destined to last forever.

As my career in speech pathology unfolded, I began to take an interest in metaphysics, an awareness of our being which is beyond physical. This is the part of us that does not show up on an MRI or EKG. I am talking here about the subtle levels of the body or the energy field. It is the part that cannot be seen, touched, smelled, or tasted through the physical realm but can be experienced with the senses as we move beyond the physical. It is the part of us that starts out as energy, becomes thought, enters awareness, and then creates something in the physical world. As children, we are naturally more connected to this aspect of ourselves. We hear it in the wise statements that our two-year-olds make and in the precise descriptions that our five-year-olds give the kindergarten teacher about what is really going on at home.

During my own childhood, I had always possessed a sixth sense about people. One time, when I was six years old, my mother had her friends over to play bridge. I said to my mother, "How come Mr. So-and-so (the husband of one of my mother's guests) is playing around with a woman who is not Mrs. So-and-so?" My mother was naturally horrified and asked where I got such a strange idea. She did not know it at the time, but the scenario turned out to be true. I have had similar intuitive experiences—thoughts, moments, or even dreams that I could not explain—throughout my childhood and into my adult life. As a child, I used to play a game with myself where I would look at someone and try to feel what they might be feeling or experiencing, only to find out later on that on several occasions my sense of them and their reality were one and the same. I always told myself, "I'll file that away as an experience I don't understand now but hope to later on." I know that, as a caregiver of a child diagnosed with autism, you undoubtedly have had many of those moments. Moments that are hard to explain, deeply touching, and confusing all at the same time.

In the mid 1990s, I became close to a woman named Ann who was attending a school that was training her to heal through recognizing and working with the body's energy system. I know this may sound a little "Left Coast," but more and more people are coming to believe that what we see isn't all there is. Highly credible writers like Deepak Chopra, Elisabeth Kübler-Ross, and Caroline Myss have put their substantial credibility and authority behind the idea that we can be harmed or healed by the way we relate to our energy. Even traditional medicine has begun to recognize that there's often more to healing than "take two pills and call me in the morning." More than a decade ago, Bill Moyers' TV series and book Healing and the Mind brought home to America the idea that you weren't necessarily kooky just because you were willing to open your mind to alternative ideas about illness and healing.

These days it seems as though a growing number of people are willing to look at life from a more spiritual standpoint. Many are noticing synchronicities in their lives, thinking about the deeper meaning of things, and generally acknowledging that what we can see is only the tip of the iceberg. Back in 1999, though, if I had talked about an awareness of energy within the speech pathology community, they would have thought that I had lost it. But my friend in energy training understood. I could talk to her about it. And that's when Riley came into my life.

I was working in a small town in Maine as a pediatric speech pathologist, and I received a call to meet a new client, a four-year-old boy, at a daycare center operating in a private home. It was a big house with a large play area downstairs and a couple of bedrooms downstairs as well, and it was in one of those rooms that I was to have my first session with Riley. The daycare provider was a man, which was somewhat unusual. His name was Stephen, and he had developed a real bond with Riley. It was obvious that he truly cared about the boy. When I saw Riley for the first time, I saw an irrepressibly cute child with brown hair cut almost in a bowl-type haircut and warm, but distant, eyes. He was repeating a phrase over and over as he marched back and forth on the linoleum: "It's the millennium! It's 1999!"

I watched Riley, and all of a sudden he came right up to me. Parents of children diagnosed with autism know that this is not typical. I didn't know that at the time, though, because I had little experience with such children. He looked me right in the eye and asked quizzically, "Master?"

I was taken aback, and I looked at him thinking, "Who's the master here? Him or me?"

There was just something about the way he looked at me. He spoke clearly, enunciating perfectly the word "master." That's just strange, I thought. At the same time, I felt awkward yet comfortable when Riley looked at me. It may sound crazy, but it felt as though he was looking right into me, right into my soul. I had that other-worldly sensation that he saw a part of me that I hadn't even seen myself.

I later learned that it can take many sessions to gain eye contact with an autistic child. Much of the traditional approach toward autism at the time was geared toward forcing eye contact, which, when you think about it, is ridiculous. Riley certainly didn't need to be forced. He just looked right at me, with all the knowing in the world radiating through those eyes.

Stephen told us we could use one of the back bedrooms downstairs so that we would not be distracted by the other children in the daycare center. Riley did not want to be in that room. I sat in front of the door and watched him, fascinated, with no idea of what to say to him. At first he was very upset to be stuck in the room, but once he realized that he wasn't going anywhere until we had a chance to get to know each other, he calmed down completely. And that's when I had the moment that changed my life. I looked at him and noticed an image floating above his body. I now understand that what I was seeing is defined as a light body. Although I had never seen anything like this before, it wasn't eerie or terrifying. Instead, I felt a deep curiosity for an experience that was beyond what I had consciously known before. I wasn't scared, but I remember thinking, "Oh my God, what is this? Why am I seeing what I'm seeing?"

We sat in the room together, and I gave him space while I tried to understand what was happening. I needed to calm down because I was so surprised and a little overwhelmed by what I was experiencing. He, on the other hand, seemed perfectly calm. By focusing on my breathing, I was able to relax. I asked myself why his energy body or his light body would be outside of him, seemingly disconnected from his physical form.

Riley continued to walk around the room, making his repetitive statements—"It's the millennium! It's 1999!" I just let him move around the room. I didn't want him to feel controlled or afraid. Finally he sat down, and I went over to him. I later learned that it's not always easy to have physical contact with autistic children—they don't like to be touched by new people. I had no idea, so I touched his ankle just to connect to him, and as I did so, I was aware that I was doing something to the energy field above him.

What exactly was I seeing? It was a cloudy, nearly transparent mass of pale yellow light that was an exact outline of Riley's physical body. It floated above him and to his right side, and it had a "tail" that dangled from the right foot of his light body to the area of his heart in his physical body. I had never seen anything like that before in my life. After I left, I wondered if I really saw something or simply imagined it.

The minute I got home, I called my friend Ann, who was a student of Barbara Brennan's School of Healing. This school taught its students the nuances of the different layers of the human energy field and how chaos in any of these layers could cause disease in the physical body. I figured that if anyone would know what I had seen, she would be the one.

"I have an energy question for you," I said, and then, too excited to let her get a word in edgewise, I described my entire meeting with Riley and the strange light I had seen.

"It was just sort of hanging there, and it didn't move except for this tail-like thing that hung down from his foot."

"His physical foot?" Ann asked.

"No, no, the foot on the body floating above him."

"Oh," she said, and then she suggested that I turn to a particular chapter of Barbara Brennan's book Hands of Light to see if that matched what I was seeing. This book was a guide to healing through the human energy field, and Barbara herself was one of the pioneers in energy awareness.

"It's right on," I exclaimed.

"You realize," Ann said carefully, "that what you saw was Riley's light body."

I tried to absorb this information. "But why was his light body hanging above him like that?"

"Because his light body is not inhabiting his physical body," Ann said, excited for me.

Now I understood what Riley was trying to tell me—not in words, because he was nonverbal except for his spontaneous utterances about the millennium and 1999, but in another way. I had received his message to me all at once as a kind of "knowing." At that moment I was not sure if that knowing was a form of telepathy or what, but in those moments of interaction with him, I was fully present and open to this incredible new experience. Riley "informed" me that he was in two different places at the same time. He could not occupy his physical body with his light body. His physical body was having one experience, and his light body was having another. The two weren't working as one. I realize now that he was asking me if I could help make that happen. And I further realize that I had agreed to do so, but with no idea of what I would be doing.

I had never before had an experience that could be defined as telepathic, and yet I knew this experience was real. In that moment I had no concern for what was happening or for my response, and I somehow simply knew that I had the skills to act on Riley's request.

Over the next few sessions, I did make some attempts to engage Riley in "appropriate" therapeutic techniques. But frankly, I wasn't sure that showing him pictures and asking him to match objects to them was actually helpful. He seemed frustrated by every activity that I thought he should try. Frequently, he would just flat out refuse, unless I signaled to him that I would indeed help him bring his light body into his physical form. In Riley's presence, I had the unusual experience of feeling that I was just following his direction. He knew what he needed. Again, who was the real master here, him or me?

In our first few sessions, I was so enthralled with the process that was unfolding that I never questioned the method. It seemed fine. Riley wasn't "asking" me to do anything that I felt was wrong or would hurt him in any way. He was asking me to gently bring his light body into his physical form. I know this has to sound odd, or perhaps even unbelievable, to anyone who has not spent time experiencing or reading about these sorts of things. If you are the parent of an autistic child, though, you surely sense that your child's energy vibrates, if you will, at a different frequency than other people's. That's just how they are: they feel different. You've also no doubt experienced your own frustration and the frustration of your child with some of the traditional approaches to autism. Even if it does seem hard or impossible to believe that these children are imploring us to recognize that healing (the integration or blending of their higher vibration into their physical form), can come through this kind of work, we can still work on finding new solutions by trying to understand them on all the levels at which they function.

To go a step further, Riley also asked me to "patch" the energetic leaks that were occurring in his body. Back then, children with autism could not hold their energy in physical form and therefore would leak energy, especially in the lower extremities and in the joints of the body. (I'll explain this in greater detail in later chapters, and I'll also explain why this is no longer the case.) It was clear just by looking at Riley that his body was like a porous container for his energy. I remember questioning if this is why children diagnosed with autism move around so much, flap their arms, or repeat words and phrases over and over again. Did they just not know what to do with the energy their bodies contain, or was it that the energy of the light body and that of the physical body were just not a match? As our sessions went forward, Riley would instruct me to put energy "band-aids" on his knees and elbows. I did so by placing my hands on his knees and then seeing the patch through my mind's eye. I watched this patching as if it were a movie playing in front of me. I could see a patch go on and in some cases watch another energy leak occur somewhere else in the body, usually at the joints and sometimes on the palms of the hands or the arches of the feet.

What did Riley's parents think of all this? To be honest, I did not share with them the energy work that was going on. At the time, I didn't really have words to explain it, and it likely would have been too weird for them to understand. They liked the results we were getting. Riley was calmer, less prone to the repetitive physical and verbal behaviors that mark autistic children, and generally happier. Their attitude was, whatever you're doing, keep on doing it.

Riley and I continued our work together. He next taught me that the high-vibrational frequency that is autism responds nicely to music and color. He was nonverbal but very telepathic, as are many of these children if we only have the ability to understand them. I found myself dreaming about him, and I realized that he was seeking to communicate with me through my dreams. He would occasionally come to me in the sleep state to give me an idea. One morning I awoke with the feeling that I should bring in colored scarves for our session and put them over him. When I did this, I was amazed. Riley liked it, and I could see the color pouring into Riley's energy field, being used where it was needed. Every color vibrates at its own frequency, and colors have been used for millennia in Eastern healing disciplines related to the body's energy. I also noticed that when we were engulfed in color, Riley would make direct, sustained eye contact with me. I had the strong sense that he was retaining information that I was giving him verbally.

Over the next few sessions, I continued to bring in scarves of various colors. Riley would choose which color scarf he needed. I could see the imprint of the color in his energy field. His body and consciousness seemed to respond to the color on multiple levels.

We continued to work on integrating his light body into his physical body. One morning, months along in our work, Riley seemed very content. He appeared to be more present than usual. I could see his presence when he looked into my eyes. When I placed my hand on his left foot, the energy came all the way in. I could see it connect with the earth. When I touched the right foot, Riley spoke his first verbal appropriate phrase to me in the entire course of our work together. "Ow! That hurts!" he exclaimed.

I immediately withdrew my hand and let the energy move back to his right ankle. The left stayed "grounded" and the right floated. With his awareness, Riley told me that it was not yet time for him to be fully in his body.

We had a few more sessions after that, and I asked him if I should tell his parents about our experiences. He told me, "They're not ready yet." Shortly after that, I stopped seeing him in therapy sessions. The commute to his town was long, and our work together seemed to come to a natural close, yet I continued to experience the repercussions of our initial meetings for several months after those sessions.

My reason for telling you about my work with Riley is to extend an invitation to you to look at the treatment of autism in an entirely new way, one that does not necessarily rely on forcing a result through pharmaceuticals, behavioral readjustment, or any of the other means by which autism has traditionally been treated. It may or may not seem credible that I have the ability to work with the energy of an autistic child as I'm describing in these pages. But surely you would agree with me that the difference in the energy of an autistic child and that of other children is palpable. If so, doesn't it make sense that working with the energy of an autistic child might offer a new and potentially exciting and successful way to understand and experience autism? If nothing else, it begs the question "What am I missing when I look at my child?"

I know this is a lot to ask you to accept at face value. Typically when I meet parents, they have the opportunity to look into my eyes and gauge my sincerity, something that's obviously not possible given the limitations of a book. You are most welcome to visit my Web site, www.Bluestarbrilliance. com, where you can see me and make up your own mind. You can see there that I look remarkably normal and do not have antennas.

Not long after I started seeing Riley, I began to build an office in my home so that I could see speech pathology clients there. As it happened, I never saw a single speech client there. By the time the space was ready, I had a fulltime healing practice with a specialty in autistic children, although all kinds of people came through those doors. I had not done any marketing or advertising. It was all from word of mouth, starting when I quietly confided in a few people and they began bringing their children to see me. Next I began sessions for parents. At one point whenever I went to the grocery store, people were seeking me out for answers and opinions. Yikes! Eventually I developed the awareness that I did not have to be physically present with a person to assist them, and that presented many new possibilities.

A year went by before I saw Riley again. His family moved into the town next to mine. Riley's mother and I had stayed in intermittent contact, so when she was close enough to resume therapy sessions, she called. I had informed her that I was no longer doing "straight" speech therapy, but that I would love to see Riley again. Riley and I resumed our sessions, and he continued to teach me new things. On July 10, as a birthday present to myself, I sat down in my office and did a distance session with Riley. I applied everything that he had taught me and directed it for his benefit. My birthday present came a day later, when I went to see Riley for our weekly session.

When I went to Riley's home, his mother told me that many of his autism-related behaviors had changed. He was enjoying his bath, which he had always hated. He was using more spontaneous words, sleeping better, interacting with his siblings, and he was now writing words. He came downstairs and looked me in the eyes. Then he took me by the hand, and his mother led us to his sister's room, where we could work in private. I was curious about his writing skills. I handed him a blank piece of white paper and a black marker. He was so present, making frequent eye contact, smiling, and being more social than I had ever seen him before. He used a combination of written words to convey his powerful message to me. Before I asked him anything, he printed across the top of the page:

ERASABLE YOUR ASABLE

I asked him if he meant that we were able to erase the condition of autism.

He wrote:

ABSOWUTELY AMAZING

I began to cry, and as the tears streamed down my face, he looked at me and smiled and wrote:

WOIVE YOU

As he wrote, he said out loud, "Love you."

Then he added:

INS MOST AMAZING VANS

And he said; "It's most amazing advance."

NOW VANS MAGIC

"Now advance magic."

◆   ◆   ◆

Riley jump-started my awareness. The many children who followed have confirmed and refined my knowledge and ability to work with energy. The skills I developed through my work have become integrated into every aspect of my life. I no longer perceive the world as I did nearly ten years ago. In the past, when I wanted to tune my awareness to the frequency that is autism, I sat quietly and meditated. After a few moments, I would feel myself moving into that energy. These days the experience is very different. The energy of autism no longer seems to be something that I have to go outside myself to acquire. I can appreciate that the concept may be hard to grasp, but I have a new experience of the energy of autism. I will never view the condition again as a "disorder." I think of autism as an energetic pattern, and I have learned to connect with various aspects of it. As a result, I have been able to help thousands of children and their families. Does autism "go away" with the approach I have been given? Yes, but not in the way you may think. There are various factors that will be discussed later that play a part in the "cure." Through this method of treatment, autistic children will not begin to look just like all the other children, because they are not here to look like all the other children. As we, their caregivers, become empowered to see beyond the limits of their physical experience into the brilliance that they offer us, new opportunities present themselves and lead you down the best possible path on their behalf.

The last time I saw Riley, I would still describe him as autistic by traditional diagnostic standards. Yet he and the children that have followed him have taught me that by making parents, educators, and therapists aware of the energy of this population, everyone can better understand, communicate with, and connect to children diagnosed with autism. I mentioned earlier in this chapter the idea that this book is an invitation to you to view the diagnosis and treatment of autism in a brand new way. The journey of raising an autistic child is one you most likely did not wish for. The parents with whom I work often feel, in the beginning, guilt over possible choices they may have made in their lives or what secrets may lie in their genetics that led to the birth of an autistic child. They are frequently ashamed of their children's behavior and are embarrassed to go to family gatherings or even the supermarket, because they are afraid that they and their children will be objects of curiosity or even ridicule and scorn. They are frequently afraid because they do not know what is the best treatment for their children, how to give them the freedom and dignity they need, which specialist to see, what approach to take. And they fear for the future of their children—what kind of life will they have as teenagers or adults?

If these are real questions in your mind, you are not alone. The good news is that there is an exciting new way—an effective, safe, and expansive way—to view and interact with autism. It may not be the journey you wished or expected to take, but I want to take it with you. Open your mind to the ideas that I'm sharing, however strange or impossible they may seem at first, and together we will journey to a place where your child will feel understood, loved, and healed as never before.

Chapter 2

A New Understanding of Autism

My experience with Riley awakened me to the knowledge that there is more to autism than meets the eye, but it was all the children and families that followed that anchored that awareness into a new reality. It was experience that changed my perception. I understand that even allowing a different experience to arise within you is difficult when the majority of people that you interact with around your child are telling you that they have a "disorder." The medical community will tell you that autism is a neurologically based disorder that causes significant difficulty in the area of communication, behavior, and socialization. They will also tell you that there is no cure. The traditional medical model will focus on what your child is not doing. I can completely understand their point of view, although I do not agree with it. There is a significant limitation in looking at autism simply through the eyes of what is not happening. By the nature of "diagnosis" the medical community has to be looking at "what is going wrong." This mindset is birthed out of a presumption that we are limited to our physical behaviors and mental abilities. This model sees only the physical manifestation and completely ignores the experience that may be occurring beyond that behavior. I can hear you saying, "Yes, but their behaviors are of primary concern, and they do impact my child's ability to participate in life."

I completely understand. I also understand that if we are not seeing the whole picture, then we could be limiting the ways to handle those behaviors. Sometimes handling the behavior is as easy as seeing beyond it.

Let me give you an example. I was hired by a family to go and see their child, Ryan, who had been diagnosed as PDD (Pervasive Developmental Delay). The doctors had told this family that their child would have difficulty forming connections to others and may have difficulty learning in a typical educational environment. I went to observe him in his Montessori school at the request of his parents because his teacher was complaining that he had become disruptive in class and she was having a difficult time managing his behavior. I watched this child sit through a preschool circle time. He sat directly in front of the teacher and the rest of the class as she began to read The Polar Express. The teacher appeared very happy, but I could feel and see something else. During the reading of the story, little Ryan began to rock back and forth and at one point reached out towards her and then retracted his hand. You can see that, when looking through the physical eyes at the situation, she could feel that he was being disruptive and maybe even a little aggressive. After the reading, the teacher and I spoke privately.

"Why were you feeling so sad as you were reading that book just now?" I asked.

"Oh, I wasn't sad. That is one of my favorite books," she replied.

I sat silent for a moment and asked if I could tell her what I sensed.

"Sure," she replied hesitantly. "I noticed that as you read your face appeared to be happy, but I could feel a deep sadness within you," I explained.

Ryan was able to feel that as well. At that point the teacher began to cry. She confessed, "That is one of my favorite books because I used to read it to my son all the time. But he's grown now, and we've had a falling out. I don't get to see him much anymore, and when I read that book, it reminds me of him."

"I can see that it hurts you deeply," I whispered.

I went on to explain to her that little Ryan, at all of four years of age, was also noticing her heartbreak and became distressed by it. He was rocking in and out of her energy in an attempt to soften it somehow. He even reached out toward her heart to try to grab out what was making her so sad, but from a strictly physical perspective, it looked like an antagonistic act.

There are many levels from which to see, and the medical and educational communities are trained to see in a certain way. Frankly, most of us are trained to see in much the same way. If you can't touch it, see it, taste it… then it must not be real. That may be true for those who have been raised to believe that, but we now have a whole population of children who do not experience the world in that way, yet we are still measuring them by our standards.

Parents are asking, "Why is there so much autism in the world, and how did it come to this?" There are many answers to that question, again based on the lens through which you choose to view the situation. The first thing to recognize is that autism did not just pop into our experience one day. As with everything else that is physical, autism was first an energy, and the experience of it has been building over time. As we discussed in the first chapter, the energy of our thoughts brings about the manifestation of things in the physical realm. This concept is being expressed throughout the media. Television programs such as The Oprah Winfrey Show and Larry King Live have done numerous shows on the power to manifest through our thoughts. Films like The Secret and What the Bleep Do We Know? have shown that like energy attracts like energy.

What do I mean that the energy of autism has been building? If like energy attracts like energy, and if, as we discussed in chapter 1, the energy of children diagnosed with autism is vibrating at a higher frequency than that of the rest of us, then what is attracting that? Let's answer that on a couple different levels. From my vantage point, the diagnosis of autism is a higher vibrational pattern than say the diagnosis of ADD/ADHD. It takes just a brief history lesson to see that the diagnosis of ADD/ADHD started minimally and then increased significantly until in some classrooms there were more children diagnosed with ADD/ADHD than were not.[1] One principal, back in 2001, called me to meet with her and discuss the rise of ADD/ADHD within her school population. She confessed that 33 percent of her population was so diagnosed. She was not sure what to do. She complained that the disruption to the previously calm state of the school was enough for her to contact someone with out-of-the-box views like me. I told her that when the percentage got to be over fifty, the whole school would change naturally to accommodate the learning needs of this new population. It was not the children that were going to change, but the systems that were going to have to change because of them. This population seemed to plateau not long after the rise of autism. Autism increased consistently, and by the mid nineties ADD/ADHD was waning as the diagnosis of choice. The children of the ADD/ADHD era were simply setting the vibrational setting for an even higher vibration of autism. We'll look at the specific gifts and talents of these populations a little later in the book.

At the same time as this increase in vibration from the ADD/ADHD population to that of autism was on the rise, so were all kinds of other factors. The rise of environmental toxins—or, perhaps more accurately, the increased saturation of our physical bodies with these toxins—became predominate as a potential cause of these "conditions." Biological factors such as environmental pollutants and food and pharmaceutical toxins were surely strong contributing factors. A strong case can be made that the toxins that we put into our children's bodies have a lot to do with what later becomes the diagnosis of autism. Books such as Jenny McCarthy's <u>Louder than Words</u> are great resources. McCarthy discusses what causes toxins in the body and how to go about reducing them through diet and modifications in the immunization schedule. Let's first discuss immunizations or, better said, vaccinations. Parents tell me all the time, "My child was talking just fine until their eighteen-month check up." The American Medical Association came out with a report in 2004 rejecting any causal association between the MMR vaccine and autism. But let's be frank, what can you expect from the American Medical Association? First, they are looking at this diagnosis through a strictly medical lens, and although they would rather not hear this, that

---

1   Between 1989 and 2000, diagnosis rates of both autism and ADHD quadrupled. David S. Mandell, Sc.D. et al., "Trends in Diagnosis Rates for Autism and ADHD at Hospital Discharge in the Context of Other Psychiatric Diagnoses," Psychiatric Services (January 2005), 56.

lens is bought and paid for by major pharmaceutical companies. At the same time that the vibration/way of being of our children is increasing so significantly, the rate and distribution of "required" vaccinations is also increasing. Hum!

A more recent study, released in January 2008, echoed the findings of the American Medical Association. "Vaccines with thimerosal and without have been safe and appropriate to give our children," said Robert Schechter, a medical officer with the Department of Health Services and lead author of the study, according to the San Francisco Chronicle of January 8, 2008. It is difficult to believe some of these studies when most are bought and paid for by Big Pharma. The government simply cannot be trusted to produce credible results when so many of the people on the government payrolls are influenced by the financial support of the pharmaceutical companies, which also represent the major source of medical research in the United States today. If you have ever felt like questioning authority, this is an awfully good place to start. Books such as Evidence of Harm by David Kirby and The Sanctity of Human Blood by Tim O'Shea are great starting places.

Chapter 3

A Mirror Reflection of the World

I know this book has been taking you in a direction that you may not have expected. Most parents, when confronted with a child diagnosed with autism, are simply looking for ways to manage the child's behavior or have the child fit in. This whole business about your child being a harbinger of a new tomorrow or a being who vibrates at a different frequency than the rest of us—I understand that that's a little bit hard to take. And yet I would be shortchanging you if all I did was offer you a recipe book for how to "get" your child to "behave right." My real role is to help you understand these higher aspects of your child and how these things play out in their daily life. Then you will see that your child is a blessing to be marveled at, an opportunity for growth and not simply a set of problems to be fixed.

When I speak to audiences about autism, I talk about it from three perspectives—evolution, potential, and awareness. In this chapter, I'd like to take you more deeply into each of these three areas with regard to the cluster of behaviors and attitudes diagnosed as autism. But before doing that, I'd like to offer some examples of other inexplicable occurrences that may help you better understand where I'm coming from and make things somewhat easier and more comfortable to grasp.

We're all familiar with extraordinary accounts of identical twins separated at birth who marry people with the same first name on the same day, who eat the same kind of breakfast cereal every morning, and who know immediately when something good or bad happens to the other without a conscious word being spoken.

And at the same time, we all have experienced a moment that could be described as clairvoyance or ESP—we knew when a child of ours was suddenly in danger, or we sensed somehow that a loved one had passed away moments before we received the phone call confirming that intuitive sense, or we had some other awareness that we could not explain away through rational means.

And then there are the "white light" experiences that have been documented by hundreds of thousands or even millions of individuals who have had near-death experiences. Some have reported seeing themselves from a vantage point above the operating table, some have experienced the white light and welcoming hands indicating the shift from this life to the afterlife, and some have described other equally amazing occurrences.

By and large, we don't doubt the reality of such a phenomenon, whether it's another remarkable story of the bond between identical twins separated at birth, our own intuition, or the near-death experience that happened to someone we read about. We do have a comfort level with such inexplicable moments, even if we don't thoroughly understand them on an intellectual level.

So it is with children diagnosed with autism. Part of their gift is the openness to have those metaphysical, or paranormal, or psychic, or whatever term is most acceptable to you, moments … all the time. It's not that they are super psychic children, but they are able to maintain a higher state of awareness all the time. They are simply functioning more from the right brain than the left. Much like members of the animal kingdom, which sense their environment, these children have a strong instinctual way of knowing, but they are trying to process and express that instinctive knowledge through cognitive thought.

The rest of us may rarely experience such "ESP" moments in a lifetime, and yet for children diagnosed with autism, such moments are a way of life. Like the rest of us, they have five senses, but they also have a sixth sense—intuition, another right brain function. They operate from this heightened sense of awareness every minute of every day. They feel and sense their way through life versus thinking their way through. They are multi-experiencers in the highest sense of the word, naturally tapped into an amazing array of multifaceted stimulation, not only from the physical environment but from more subtle energy patterns that most of us miss because we are so caught up in our left-brain concepts of what is real. Along with the rise in the number of diagnoses of autism in recent years has been an even greater rise in the number of children diagnosed with ADD, Attention Deficit Disorder, or ADHD, Attention Deficit Hyperactivity Disorder. These children have a hard time focusing intellectually, which can drive teachers and parents batty, but it's because they are distracted by their own ability to read energy, to notice things on more subtle levels that the rest of us rarely notice. Children with ADD or ADHD aren't stupid. Far from it! They too are simply using more right-brain skills. But what drives them to distraction is the fact that they can see … and feel … so much more than the rest of us. That's their gift.

Children diagnosed with autism take things a step further. Just as identical twins can reflect back energy and information to each other without words, and in the most amazing ways, so do children diagnosed with autism reflect back to us information about how we are feeling, also on an intuitive, unspoken level. I like to think of them as a clear reflective mirror to the world.

Let me give you an example. One time I was working with a child, a little boy who had been diagnosed with autism, in his family's home. He began to cry spontaneously for no apparent reason. When I asked him what was wrong, he used what method of communication he could, and he took my hand and led me to the closed master bedroom door. We knocked and entered, and sure enough, his mother, who was sitting on the bed, was on the telephone, crying.

"Your son knew you were crying," I said.

"That's amazing," the boy's mother said. "I just found out that our occupational therapist was no longer going to be able to work with him. I just got so frustrated and sad because we've gone through so many therapists, and now we're going to have to start over with someone else. Why is my son so upset? How did he even know about it?"

"He didn't know about the 'why' of why you were upset," I explained. "But he was able to sense your pain, from clear across the house. He responded by communicating your sadness to me the only way he could. He began to cry."

"What can I do to make him feel better?" his mother asked.

"You already have," I said. "You explained why you were upset, so he was able to calm down. Children diagnosed with autism have a hard time containing their own feelings when people around them, especially the people they love, are feeling strong emotion. These children are connected to others, especially family, as if they are all one. Because you were able to tell him what was going on, he was able to calm himself down."

He was able to do this without drugs, forced eye contact, or any other mechanical means of "treating" autism, I might add. Obviously there can be more to calming behaviors than in this example, but when we don't know how our children really function, then we typically offer much more "medicine" for the situation than is actually needed.

Mother and child hugged, and I had yet one more illustration of how children diagnosed with autism truly can be understood as a clear mirror to their world. They feel what we feel, and when we identify our own emotions and can explain our reasons for feeling upset to them, they can relax. For those of you who say my child won't understand those emotion words, I agree. They may not understand the words (left brain), but they will sense the balance that those words bring you (right brain) and reflect that back accordingly.

This kind of connection is not limited to physical proximity. Example: Gabriel was in a self-contained preschool classroom. He had a diagnosis of autism, and during his class time, he would frequently become extremely agitated. He would spend long periods of time during the day perseverating on his mother. Where was she? What was she doing? When would she be back? He would also have "conversations" with her. "Mommy when are you coming? Are you all right?" Looking at physical reality only, it would appear that he was becoming agitated for no reason, speaking to the unseen and basically making no sense at all based on what was going on in his immediate environment. The bigger picture looked something like this: Gabriel's mother had not one but two children with this diagnosis, and it was taking its toll on her. On the outside she would appear to be holding it all together, doing the best she could, and on the inside she was falling apart. He would act out her inner agitation at school to release the built-up energy. Thus, Gabriel would talk to her verbally from a distance, express concern for her well-being, and perseverate on where she was and when she would return. The teacher and I would smile when his mother would mention that on certain days that she felt much better handling things than on others. Her good days were the same days that her son spent releasing energy and talking to her from afar.

With that as introduction, let's talk about autism in terms of evolution, potential, and awareness. In terms of evolution, I believe these children are here to demonstrate to us new states of being, new states of how we interact with the world. When we understand their ability to be in the oneness, we can see that they can do what the rest of us haven't been ready to do. They sense things at a feeling level. It's not so much about the mind for them. It's not so much about the physical environment. They are pointing the way to the next phase in human evolution, when we go from an over-reliance on our intellect, which doesn't often get us very far, to a reliance on our ability to sense and to feel our way through all of life's situations. In some ways, that is what has been happening to you already just by having a child that does not fit into the box of society. You are naturally beginning to learn those feeling skills.

What does this mean on a practical level, I hear you asking. Within my own family structure, how can this be applied? Am I somehow responsible for all my child's negative behaviors? Our outer life is always reflecting our inner life. Sometimes the reflection is of our personal inner life and sometimes the collective inner life. There is one sure way to know the difference. If the behavior you are witnessing is aggravating you, then there is an opportunity there to clear something up personally. If it does not bother you, it's not personal. Before you start blaming yourself for every behavior that your child exhibits, please know that your child is not just reflecting your inner feelings but the feelings of everyone in the household, those whom he encounters outside the home, and in some cases the collective mass consciousness.

That's why I say, if the behavior is not hitting a personal nerve, then it is not yours. Also realize that as a culture we are taught from day one to function from the left brain. We learn the concepts of right and wrong based on societal norms. We learn to place our happiness or lack of it outside of ourselves, and we are taught to react to a situation by doing something about it versus responding by being with the situation. We are taught to deaden our feelings as if some feelings are bad and others are good. So this is more about having the opportunity to start feeling and thus experiencing life versus just thinking about how to get through the next day. I know that each of you reading this can clearly say that you have felt more raw emotion since your child was diagnosed than ever before.

In addition to reflecting your inner feelings, your children also reflect back when you have "got it," when you have understood their message as in the following example: One of my clients had been toying with the idea of taking her son out of public school. She felt that the school system was not meeting his needs. Her son's behavior was increasingly difficult in the classroom. Teachers, administrators, and therapists grew more frustrated with the child's seeming regression. As my client began to explore other options and talk to people about home schooling, her son began to "check out" at school. His behaviors started to diminish, but he wasn't actively participating at school either. Once she became enthusiastic about pulling her son out of school to homeschool him, his behaviors began to naturally change. She found that he was singing old songs that he used to love, and he began playing more and asking questions about people who had been in his life at other times when he was staying at home with mom all day.

My client had minimally told her son what she was thinking about doing. His limited verbal skills did not allow him to ask questions based on what he was sensing, but his negative behaviors at school clearly reflected her frustration with the system. When she decided that she should withdraw him from public school and look at other alternatives, he went into a world of his own, and when she made a new choice, he demonstrated his enthusiasm by singing again. His mom could see clearly that she had made a great choice; she felt the joy and so did he. She got the seal of approval from her son, and they are moving forward. You can see that if we never put together his ability to reflect the emotional energy of his environment, then we think his behaviors are separate in and of themselves. With this population, separation is the furthest thing from the truth.

Maybe now you are beginning to see why fixing the behavior is not the best method. Just like taking a pill for a headache, we can make the behavior go away in the short run, but we'll never know the cause. We'll also miss the opportunity that the moment presents by spending our energy trying to get the behavior to go away rather than finding a deeper meaning from the experience.

On another practical level, how different things would be if these same techniques were used within a husband-and-wife relationship. Instead of placing blame on the behavior of our spouse, we could recognize it as an opportunity to learn about something within our subconscious belief system. This creates the opportunity to work things out rather than add to the energy of negativity. Your family situations are stressed enough caring for your children and meeting the demands of unbelievable schedules with therapists, doctors, educators, and the like. Every moment is an opportunity, and no one knows that more than your precious child.

◆   ◆   ◆

Imagine if everyone operated on the same high level of feeling and awareness as do children diagnosed with autism. We would have a whole new way of being in the world. Children diagnosed with autism demonstrate so beautifully that they function from a feeling state. When they know that the people in their world feel whole, they feel better. And so can we all, if we follow their lead. In other words, children diagnosed with autism represent the next step in the spiritual evolution of mankind: they have moved from a predominant thinking state to a state of just being in the energy of the situation and feeling it through. Now let's turn to the issue of potential and see what that change in evolution will mean for the rest of us.

Imagine if individuals evolved to the point where our entire society was made up of people who could sense at this deep level. Perhaps we could stop something going on in the world, stop it cold in its tracks, because it feels bad, instead of waiting for it to manifest as a physical war or a terrorist attack. If you had three hundred million people operating at a sensing level, instead of just the level of thinking and reacting, the potential for harmony and awareness would exist as never before. If you can sense something about me at a vibrational level, and you can help me through it, the potential is less about separation and more about interconnectedness. When we deal with situations before they become physical, we alleviate so much unnecessary suffering.

That's what children diagnosed with autism do, day in, day out. But if we don't know what they're doing, if we don't realize that they are reacting to the environment in such a different way than the way we were taught, we say, "That's weird! That's not right! They have to be made right!" Yet in reality, we are simply looking at them through lower-vibration eyes.

So far, we've talked about children diagnosed with autism in terms of what they represent for human evolution and for the potential for change in the way we interrelate, not only in our homes, but also in our society as a whole. Now let's turn to the third area under discussion in this chapter, the concept of awareness.

What else is there to the potential that these children offer the world? We all know that animals have a heightened sense of agitation before natural catastrophes such as earthquakes or floods. Children diagnosed with autism possess that same instinctual ability, not to predict experiences but to sense them as they arise. And there's not an autism teacher out there who would deny the fact that children diagnosed with autism cycle with the moon, which is also a vibrational pull. How much happier and more secure would our society be if people related to the everyday world with the same heightened awareness that the animal kingdom experiences natural disasters? If everybody could sense and feel what was going on, they would move naturally in their lives toward things that would bring them joy and away from those which would cause them pain. We would have the potential for a happier, less fragmented society. We would all experience subtle levels of knowing without having to speak about things, a knowing that's beyond words. We would see that our perceived personal problems are not personal at all, but collective in nature.

That's why traditional school doesn't work for children diagnosed with autism. It's a left-brained, physical, and mental approach to learning, whereas these kids are oriented for a right-brained, vibration, feeling, and imagery approach. Obviously we need both, but unless we all realize that this other aspect even exists, how can we create an appropriate learning environment for these children? Creating a suitable learning environment where children diagnosed with autism can truly flourish is the topic of another book altogether.

When I talk to the parents of children diagnosed with autism about this heightened awareness, they don't react as if I am speaking from some sort of metaphysical never-never land. Instead, they completely understand what I'm talking about. They've already experienced the fact that their children seem to spend a lot of time out of their bodies, as if they were vibrating too high to be in them. They've sensed that their children possess some sort of awareness, that sixth sense we talk so much about, going beyond the physical senses, but they've never understood what it meant. I'm basically putting words to the music that's been in parents' heads for some time.

It often happens that grandparents, who have a slightly smaller emotional connection or sense of responsibility to their grandchildren than do parents to their own children, get what I'm saying even more quickly. Grandparents frequently say, "That makes so much sense! I see him do that all the time!"

Let me give you an example. I was giving a workshop on the gifts of autism. An older couple sat and listened carefully to all that I have explained to you here, and when I talked about how the children will sometimes just sob for no apparent reason, a lovely grandmother in the audience began to weep. She said, "My grandbaby cries for her mother. She cries because she can feel the overwhelm in her mother's heart." I suggested that this amazingly wise woman return to her grandchild and tell her that she understands. I did not hear from her again, but history would tell me that the "grandbaby" became a lot less tearful just sensing that someone understood what she was reflecting.

These children have an amazing ability to deliver "aha!" moments not only to parents and grandparents but to the rest of us as well. I remember one time working with a teacher who had four or five children in her classroom, and one of them, the most adorable little boy you've ever seen, with big blue eyes and dark hair, couldn't stop abusing the teacher. He was hitting, kicking, spitting, but only acting out with the teacher, not with the other children, the paraprofessionals in the classroom, or with me.

"This is making me so mad," the teacher said. "Why is he only doing this to me?"

I asked, "In what ways are you beating yourself up? Is it possible that he's reflecting back to you what you do to yourself?"

As you can imagine, the teacher wasn't very happy with my question at first, but then she started nodding. "I do that all the time!" she admitted. "I beat myself up mercilessly!"

These are the reflections that children diagnosed with autism offer all the time. It's great when you can get a handle on it, and it's terribly upsetting to parents when they can't. This is the extraordinary awareness that these children offer the rest of us.

Evolution, potential, awareness. These are three more of the gifts of autism. As a parent, you're almost undoubtedly saying, "I never signed on for any of this! It all sounds very exciting the way you put it, but I just wish I had a normal kid!"

Don't beat yourself up for having feelings like that. Virtually every parent of a child diagnosed with autism with whom I've ever worked has expressed the same feelings. Or they've had the same feelings and couldn't bring themselves to admit it. I understand that this feels like more than you've signed on for. But when you see your child as the amazing being that he or she is, brought down to earth gifted with these extraordinary abilities and awarenesses, this might be the moment when you begin to understand why I redefine autism as "Awesomism."

Because these children are awesome. And as a loving parent who wants the best for your child, so are you.

Chapter 4

How the Autistic Child Experiences the World

The approach to experiencing life through vibrational energy is foreign to most parents of children diagnosed with autism. These parents, like most adults in our society, tend to look at the world in rational or intellectual terms. We create a mental construct based on information we receive through words or pictures. We see something, read something, or hear something, and act accordingly.

However, there is more to "knowing" than the sort of book learning, learning in college classes, or other forms of intellectual "knowing" that exist in our world. Children diagnosed with autism have a heightened sense of awareness or acuity that the rest of us possess to a more limited degree. In the Dr. Seuss movie Horton Hears a Who, Jim Carrey, as Horton, knows that something exists beyond what is physically present. His ability to hear beyond the frequency of others allows him to be open to a whole new reality and experience a reality beyond what others perceive. Such is the experience with children diagnosed with autism. The kangaroo, played by Carol Burnett, is the archetype of typical human awareness.

When faced with Horton's awareness, she asserts, "If you can't see it or touch it, it can't be real."

We adults are comfortable with the way we think—we like our mental constructs, our intellectual understandings of the world. They're safe for us, and they help us make sense of what would otherwise be a bewildering experience, namely, life itself. So it's often hard for any of us, let alone parents of children diagnosed with autism, to accept the idea that our children experience more of the world than we do. Sometimes, we even fear that they experience more, because it is not within our comfort zone. It is not for us to change their experience but to have a greater understanding of it. Just as Horton in the movie brings a connection between the world of the Whos and his jungle friends, so too can we bridge the gap between what our children experience and what we currently think is true.

At this point, I hear parents saying, "But Suzy, the behaviors my child exhibits are physical!" "That's right," I respond. The behaviors are physical. But that physical behavior reaction is simply a manifestation of an underlying reality. That underlying reality is a high-vibrational energy poured into or experienced by a human being. The heightened vibrations to which children diagnosed with autism are sensitive trigger those physical reactions. If we understand that, we can work with those behaviors in a much easier way, a more subtle way, to bring about significant change. Sometimes it is so easy that just seeing the behaviors for what they are can cause them to stop. In the aforementioned movie, Horton appears to others to be absolutely crazy. He talks to things that others can't see, protects something that appears to be a simple clover as if the world depended on it (the world of the Whos does depend on it) and generally appears to the world as if he is "disordered."

It is understood that individuals who have a deficit in one physical sense compensate by having a stronger ability in another sense. It's as true with human beings as it is with other members of the animal kingdom. People who are blind often have greater hearing acuity than the average person, and conversely, people who are hearing-impaired often, but not always, have better eyesight than others. And so it goes throughout the various senses. Imagine, if you will, an individual who goes through life with all five senses at that higher level of awareness.

That, in a nutshell, is what it's like to experience the world if you are a person diagnosed with autism. The five senses are heightened and the sixth sense of awareness and knowing is predominant.

The physical hearing of children diagnosed with autism is very sensitive. They don't like loud sounds, because the volume on their hearing mechanism is already turned up very high. That's why they react so strongly and so negatively to loud sounds. Try whispering to your child, and see what happens. He will become alert, attentive and connected. When you speak in a regular volume, he has to shut you out a bit to feel comfortable. By whispering, you are honoring his highly sensitive sensory system, and he will reward you accordingly.

Their physical sense of touch is also exaggerated so that feeling the grass beneath their feet can feel like walking on millions of individual tiny fibers that move and shift under them. Movement, when you are not fully in your body, can feel fluid instead of solid. Like a drug-induced trip. No wonder these children are cautious when they touch new things.

Their sense of taste is also more sensitive than that of the rest of us. Many children are finicky eaters, but children diagnosed with autism take finicky to a new level. They tend to eat the same thing over and over again—they find something that tastes good and has a texture that they like, and they only want that. Often, the choice they make is junk food that may not be especially good for them. For some reason, they find such foods a match for their vibrating system. Unfortunately, those who prefer sugar or white flour can become addicted to such substances easily, because their systems are so clear and pure. What's it like to taste food from the perspective of a child diagnosed with autism? Imagine having a sugar or caffeine buzz because you ate a few too many cookies or drank too much coffee. The buzz that you experience in those moments is how they experience most of their sense perception all the time. It's like being electrically over-charged. That sensation is how they experience much of life, not just taste. Everything is exaggerated. Some people resort to drugs to attempt this effect. Most children are familiar with the buzzing sensation within their bodies, and that's why they often gravitate toward sugary treats, because such foods give them a heightened sense of what they already experience. This is also why gluten- and casein-free diets can be successful in reducing their exaggerated behaviors. When the buzz is reduced, it's easier to be in the body, and connections can be made.

Whatever the sensory mode of experience in the world, a child diagnosed with autism experiences things on a more expansive, exaggerated level than the rest of us. How does this manifest in terms of human relations? On a physical level, they often have to shut down their interactions with others, because the sensory overload is too much for their delicate systems. On a sixth-sense level though, they are not missing a trick. It's as though they are saying through their behavior, "I know what's going on with you and in my environment because I can feel what's going." Why do they often seem so upset when nothing outwardly appears to be wrong? Well, you'd be upset, too, if you felt and saw every sensation as they do. They often are unable to block out emotions or other data or sensory input that the rest of us find disturbing and need to block out so that we can function. Those of us who are not diagnosed with autism possess a filter that we can use in order to block out overstimulating sensations. Children diagnosed with autism have no such filter. They are expansive in their awareness of everything that they experience, and that expansiveness can be very overwhelming for a person just learning to navigate life in a little body. Therefore, any sensation that enters their experience reverberates or perseverates until they have some way of completing that experience. To these children, perseveration means working energy down from the vibrational level to the emotional level to the physical level to anchor it. This can take several attempts.

They do the same with feelings because they perpetually live in the moment. They don't stay stuck in the past, reflecting on negative emotions or negative experiences from days, months, or even years before, as do we "rational" or "normal" people. That is a function of the left brain. They get closure, and they get it in an instant—usually as soon as the incident is over. Often the emotion will appear to continue, but that has more to do with the adult projecting their feeling onto the child or continuing to feel discomfort, which the child then acts out. Example: One of my friends took her child to the park to play. When they got there, he wanted to play with a ball. My friend had not brought the ball, felt horrible and felt even worse when her son cried for the one thing she had forgotten. After a short time, he found something else to enjoy and was very happy. His mother, however, spent the rest of the afternoon looking for the ball to bring him happiness, which he already felt. When she finally found the ball and offered it to him, surprise, he had no interest in playing with it. So the easiest way to "manage" the behavior of a child diagnosed with autism is to be aware of our own emotional state. If we can go through life with a little bit more calm and clarity, so will they.

The dominant emotion I encounter among parents of children diagnosed with autism is guilt. Parents feel guilty, as we have discussed, because they believe their genetics, their choices, or some other actions or inactions they have taken have led to the diagnosis of autism in one or more of their children. Sometimes there is guilt and frustration for simply not being able to figure it all out. But the reality is that parents don't cause autism! When we demonstrate our feelings of guilt to others, it's often because we're looking to others to resolve those feelings for us, to give us some sort of externally based permission to stop feeling guilty. But by bringing guilt into an encounter with a child diagnosed with autism, we're looking to that child to resolve our feelings of guilt, usually by trying to get those obvious behaviors to stop. Please hear me when I say that those behaviors are NOT a reflection of what you did wrong. They are simply a mirror of how you are feeling about their behavior. Unfortunately, the medical model for treating autism is not all that interested in understanding how the child diagnosed with autism experiences the world vibrationally. Instead, the medical model is all about making adults comfortable by finding ways, often through force or medication, to stop an autistic child's behavior. By now, I think you'll agree that this approach is folly. The medical model limits potential and doesn't aid the child diagnosed with autism. As discussed earlier, there are ways to make it easier for your highly aware child to be here and experience life, but suppressing feelings and behavior doesn't do anyone any good, autistic or not. When you think about it, that entire approach is based in fear. The parents fear how others, in any social setting from a family party to a trip to the supermarket, will view the child ... and the parent, too. Parents, understandably, find the diagnosis of autism itself frightening, and they find the behaviors of their children diagnosed with autism equally frightening. So it's understandable that fear would be such an important part of the equation.

The solution is not about suppression of emotion—that of the parent or the child. Instead, it's about moving the parent gently from a place of fear to a place where he or she can have a new level of awareness about who their child is, what the child is experiencing, and why it's okay. My purpose, when I work with parents, is to help them experience something beyond what the traditional authorities have told them is true. My role is to share with the parents a sense of self-empowerment, awareness, and inner knowing. That's my gift to the parents of children diagnosed with autism—the ability to trust themselves so much that they are willing to take a stand for the potential of their children and not simply accept the limitations that the medical model thrusts upon children diagnosed with autism and their parents as well. There is always potential for growth in every situation. That's the nature of life. If you are a parent of a child diagnosed with autism, or if you are a professional who works with these children, it is my goal that you see the potential sitting right there in front of you. The child diagnosed with autism experiences the world on a more expansive level than the rest of us. Instead of suppressing the child's energy, let's understand it, work with it instead of against it and unlock their potential, because they, uniquely, have the power to change consciousness and give us all a new direction in life. To paraphrase the aphorism about motherhood, the hand that rocks the cradle of the child diagnosed with autism is the hand that has the ability to rock the world.

Let's talk more about how children diagnosed with autism experience the world in an auditory manner. How do they hear differently from others? The simple answer is that they can hear sounds from several rooms away in the same house in ways that the rest of us cannot. You can have the music on in the living room and be conversing in low tones, and a child diagnosed with autism playing somewhere else in the house will be able to pick up on the tenor of your conversation. Most people wouldn't even be able to hear you talking, let alone understand the emotional content underlying your words. But that's where children diagnosed with autism are different. They can hear you, even from a distance, and they understand.

Typically, when children diagnosed with autism grasp that they are the subject of my conversations with the adults in their life, they'll come into the room, sit down next to me or on my lap, and give me a smile. I always say, "Yes, I'm telling your parents all your secrets!"

The child diagnosed with autism will laugh or give me a gesture that says, "That's okay." The child is letting me know that he or she appreciates what I'm telling the parents. Children diagnosed with autism share at least one thing in common with everyone else on the planet—they just want to be understood. They are different, not disordered; right-brained dominant, not left. Their frustration is triggered when they have the feeling that the adults in their lives—their parents, health professionals, teachers, or others—don't get them. That means, when they feel a disconnection energetically or a separation, then they have to reflect that back by being "distant." They just want to feel connected. The more you "get" them, the easier your relationship will be with them. Hopefully this information is bringing you a little closer to that understanding.

One more thing about your child's ability to "hear" a conversation from several rooms away: he or she is doing more than just hearing. The child is perceiving the entire nature of the exchange from a broader perspective. So let's use this awareness for a win-win situation. Your words carry a vibration. Negative words carry negative vibration. Positive words carry positive vibration. What do you want your child to reflect back to you, the label of disordered or the label of gifted in a new way? One of the statements that I frequently hear from parents is, "He is so manipulative." I would like to dispel this notion here and now. Your child may be perceived as manipulative, but from my vantage point they are simply attempting to bring about a new awareness. They are using all the skills they have naturally and the ones that they learn to affect their environments. Instead of "He is so manipulative," maybe we can change that statement to "He is ingenious" or "He is trying so hard to have us understand him."

Try a little test. Say these sentences to yourself as if you were saying them about yourself. I know that you will be able to "feel" these statements in your body, and I know that the negative ones will not feel good and the positive ones will feel softer. Knowing that your child picks up on the flavor of the words and the sensations that go along with them, you can quickly see that by changing the vibration of your words, you will get a very different reflection back from your child. This takes some practice because we are used to reacting versus responding. The vibration of communication is a powerful tool. Use it to your advantage, and choose your words wisely. Below are some terms that I hear frequently, and some higher vibrations of the same word. You choose what feels better.

Old Negative Labels	New Positive Labels
Demanding	Persistent
Irrational	Creative/Right-brained
Manipulative	Ingenious/Charismatic
Obstinate	Not Easily Swayed
Resistant	Focused (on creating change)

Chapter 5

Understanding the Behaviors of Children Diagnosed with Autism

Before we begin this chapter, I want to remind you once again that your children's behavior will always be first and foremost based on energy. Remember that they are vibrational beings, and that vibration can be worked with, by seeing the behaviors for what they are, or worked against, by continually adding negative energy and perceptions to the mix.

Of course, most parents are fearful, upset, and often guilt-ridden about the behavior of their children. What parents often don't realize is that they may be exacerbating or prolonging the very behavior they are trying to eliminate. Once you understand what the child is saying or doing, the behavior tends to normalize itself. It's really the law of attraction—whatever you focus on grows. There's a reason why the child diagnosed with autism behaves the way he or she does. As you gain awareness of the energy of their behaviors, you can find a way to normalize them in your own eyes, and the child will naturally have the tendency to do less of it. Let's take a look at the typical behaviors of autistic children and seek to understand what they mean, what's really going on. If you can understand the behavior, it will no longer be so frightening or upsetting. If the child feels understood, the child will feel less need to practice those particular behaviors. As your awareness increases, so does your vibration, and as your vibration increases, your vibration-driven child feels more comfortable in their environment.

Let's first consider toe walking. Children diagnosed with autism will often walk on their toes instead of walking flat-footed. It looks very different, and it sets the child apart from other children and thus becomes a disturbing trait in the eyes of the parent. What does toe walking really mean? It all comes back to energy. If you think about the child diagnosed with autism on an energy level, then you'll recognize that they have an energetic body in addition to their physical body. Remember Riley, the boy we met in chapter 1? Riley was the first child I noticed whose energetic body was completely detached from his physical body. It was literally suspended in space over his physical body. I know that sounds hard to grasp, but consider this: When a child is toe walking, it's because his energetic body is moving up and out of his physical body. If his physical body could come up into the air and levitate, it would. But the law of gravity governs the physical body in ways that it does not govern the energetic body. So when your child is toe walking, it's because his or her energy is lifting up and up and up, and this is a physical manifestation of that energetic experience.

This concept may be difficult to grasp, but it's not so different from adults' so-called normal emotional reactions. We all have moments of fright or excitement. At times like that, we can feel so excited that we can't even contain our emotions. If you think of emotions as energy, sometimes our emotions are so powerful, so energy-filled, that they overwhelm us. So we say things like, "I was beside myself." How can you be beside yourself? Only if your physical body and your energetic body can separate. And they do at times of great stress, excitement, upset, or fear. When the child diagnosed with autism feels a high level of energy shooting through him, his energetic body separates and moves upwards. That's why he toe walks. He is not really beside himself with emotion—he is "over" himself with emotion. Or better said, the emotion of fear, stress, excitement, or upset is not a match for his vibration or energetic body, and so the light (energetic) body begins to separate from the physical body.

The good news about understanding toe walking in this manner, by comparing it to the concept of being "outside ourselves," is that it makes the behavior understandable. Remember that the child diagnosed with autism wants to feel connected energetically. He is not saying, "Please understand me," on a conscious level, but is functioning at a vibrational level where he desires to feel connected or understood vibrationally, not intellectually. If you don't experience toe walking as a frightening behavior, neither will your child. It may not feel comfortable at first to look at this behavior in this manner. But the more you practice doing so, the calmer your child will be, and the briefer the period of disturbance that your child will experience. Try this the next time that you observe your child toe walking. Instead of reacting negatively internally or externally, simply move your awareness into yourself. Calm yourself and gently see your energy in your body all the way down to your toes, grounded into the earth. It may take a couple of tries at first, but most of the time your child will lower his feet and become "connected" again. This happens because as you feel connected so does he, and as you model how to connect, he follows suit.

Now let's turn to the spinning and flapping—typical movements of children diagnosed with autism. We want to think about it not in terms of some sort of physical dysfunction but in terms of processing energy. When spinning in a circle or flapping her arms, your child is simply processing a huge amount of energy passing through at that moment. What's it like to be struck by lightning? Few people can really tell us, but those who have survived the experience often speak of a huge amount of energy passing through their body. Children diagnosed with autism are prone to experiencing such lightning bolts of energy passing through their systems on a regular basis. This energy is like a pulsating, consistent stream of energy that goes in bursts and starts—like a star that comes into being, burns brightly, and then fizzles out, and then another one comes, and another one.

Is it something to be afraid of? Of course not! It's just what they do when they feel all that energy. As a parent, you are not causing that behavior. But ask yourself how you typically react when your child engages in such behavior. Does it honestly frighten you? If it does, you're not alone. It frightens most parents. It's disturbing and upsetting to see a child seemingly out of control. But now you know why the child is behaving in this manner—she is simply processing a "lightning bolt" of energy. This "lightning bolt" can be caused by a variety of things, but typically they are caused by electromagnetic shifts occurring on the planet, and those who are sensitive feel these as a surge of vibration that flows through them and then passes. If you convey your understanding of the process instead of your fear, the child will respond to your calming influence and will slow down and even cease the behavior in a much shorter time than you might ever have imagined. This is not unlike when a child falls and hurts himself and is surprised and shocked by the experience. If you add drama to the experience, then the emotion is heightened, but if you react in a calm, matter-of-fact manner, the child does not experience undue stress.

Your child can sense whether you are reacting with fear, which is obviously based on lack of understanding, or awareness of what she is really going through. You don't need words to convey your emotional state—the child diagnosed with autism, even more than the average child, can pick up on your emotions. So stay calm. Stay grounded. This will help your child understand that you "get" her. Is it a blessing or an affliction to be "struck" with this level of intense energy? That's not for me to say. My belief is that it's a good thing, or it wouldn't be happening, and it wouldn't be happening for increasing numbers of children. This is just one of the ways our planet is increasing its vibrational frequency and thus the potential consciousness of all of us. But since it is happening, respond with understanding and love, instead of fear and shame, and watch what happens.

Let's talk more about spinning. Why do children diagnosed with autism spin? If they could put it in words, they would tell you this: "I've got a lot of electrical energy moving through me, so I'll spin it off." Their process is like the process by which energy is generated at a power plant—it spins through coils on its way to becoming usable. Your child is just spinning off current. It seems odd, but it's nothing to be frightened about.

Another behavior of children diagnosed with autism is inappropriate conversation. Remember Riley marching around and repeating over and over again, "It's the millennium! It's 1999!" The best way I can explain this phenomenon is that Riley's radio, perhaps like your child's, is dialed to a different frequency. A lot of times you'll hear children speaking nonsense words. It's not nonsense to them! They're simply tuned in to a frequency higher than ours. My belief is that they are communicating at a different level from that of the "normal" person.

These children are used to communicating beyond words, and they use words that they have heard on TV and spoken by others again through repetition to convey a message. This is their way of taking their energetic knowing and trying to bring it down vibrationally from energy/vibration, through the mental and into the physical act of speaking. It is no wonder that the message can seem very broken. This is why it is so important to feel the message they are giving versus listening to it word for word.

There's nothing to be gained from punishing children who communicate on a different level. It's just their process. Let them do it, and let them do it without fear of correction, and before long there will be real communication between you..

Let's now talk about the concept of "stimming," a shorthand way of saying self-stimulating, another form of repetitive behavior. The technical term for this behavior is stereotypy, but instead of speaking in scientific jargon, let's talk about it in a way that you, as a parent of an autistic child, can readily understand. Have you ever seen a child roll a toy car thirty times off a table, watch it fall, pick it up, and then do it again? And again? And again? This is a typical behavior for children diagnosed with autism, and quite frankly, it drives most parents nuts! Why do they have to do that over and over again? Why can't they just do something else? The real question, of course, underlying all these other questions, is this: Why can't my kid be normal?

We're not really here to talk about "normal." We're here to talk about the reality of life as experienced by the child diagnosed with autism. You and I exist in a world where time is a linear concept. Things have beginnings, middles, and ends. We go to the store, we buy a cup of coffee, we drink the coffee, we throw out the cup, and we're done. Experience began, experience ended. Simple, right?

It's not so simple for the child diagnosed with autism. These children do not experience life in such a linear fashion. They don't have that same concept of beginning, middle, and end. Are they slow learners? No, they're brilliant learners. Nonlinear processing is a gift of the right hemisphere. Again, not disordered but different. These children are what I call learners beyond time. The trouble for them is that when you take someone who functions beyond time and put them into a time-space reality, the two systems do not work so well together. The outcome at a functional level is repetitive behaviors that are their attempt to grasp and function in time. For them, the concepts of past and future are difficult to understand. Because they vibrate at such a high frequency, they live in the moment the way all of the books about living in the moment, experiencing the "now," and so on, attempt to teach us adults to do. Children diagnosed with autism live in the moment in a manner to which the rest of us can only aspire. They have all possibilities and all frequencies available to them, whereas we just see what's in front of us and live in those limits. So why do they practice those repetitive behaviors? It's because they're trying to understand and experience in time and space the way the rest of us already understand things. They are trying to move their right-hemisphere experiences into a left-hemisphere reality. That's bound to look a little funky to us who know little about right-brain awareness.

Let's go back to the child diagnosed with autism rolling a toy car off a table. He's trying to integrate the concept of "this is what happens when a car falls off a table" into his mind. You or I may only need to see that car falling off the table one time. That's because we are able to attach the concepts of beginning, middle, and end to the experience the first time we see the thing happen. The beginning: you roll the car. The middle: it's falling. The end: it's on the floor. Because we don't live in the now, because we are so comfortable with the concepts of past, present, and future, we only need to see that car roll and hit the floor once for us to understand the concept: roll car, car falls, car hits floor. By contrast, the child diagnosed with autism experiences the world in a never-ending series of nows. It's now, and now it's now, and now it's now again! If they're going to attach concepts of past, present, and future to an event, it's going to take them some effort. That's why it takes the child thirty times through an experience when it would take someone who vibrates in linear time just one experience.

As the spiritual teacher Eckhart Tolle discusses in his books The Power of Now and The New Earth, the now is all there is. These children live in the now constantly, yet their perception of the now is not based on a physical reality or a mental construct but on a reality that extends beyond the physical realm. Those sensations can come from being up and out of their body and connected to more subtle energies (those metaphysical things that most of us do not experience).

They are trying to integrate that past-present-future model of thinking into their now-now-now way of being.

If the preceding explanation seems too "out there," just take away this thought: Nothing bad is happening when your child practices repetitive behaviors. It's just a demonstration of a different way of experiencing the world. Tell yourself, "It's just what my child does. I don't have to attach a negative judgment to it. I don't have to look at it through the lens of fear, guilt, shame, or embarrassment. It's my child's process. I love my child, and I may not entirely understand it, but I can live comfortably with it." If you can live comfortably with it, you will increase your child's comfort level as well. And that's going to make everything easier. Vibration is everything to these children. Increasing the vibration of their environment increases their ability to be more fully present here, which means better integration of the light body into the physical body and better connection between the right and left hemispheres. Anybody who has ever experienced a moment of their child being fully present, a moment when your child looks right at you and you can see them behind their eyes, can confirm the power of that connection. It really packs a punch!

A similar behavior to spinning and flapping is when children extend their fingers really wide. In the abstract, it looks odd. But when we consider what it means in terms of energy, it can begin to make sense. If you think of this behavior as energy moving down the child's body, along her arms, and out her fingertips, it makes sense. If you're open to this hypothesis, try it out the next time your child behaves in this manner. If you go from being disturbed by a behavior to dropping your emotional attachment to the fear and concern that you feel, the behavior will occur less frequently.

Keep in mind that you have a very high-vibrational being, a child diagnosed with autism, trying to be fully embodied in a physical form. Her job here on Earth is to be a high-vibration being. Sometimes the energy that children diagnosed with autism experience is just too overwhelming for them. Actually, that can be true for all of us. If you come from love and understanding instead of fear, guilt, or shame, you will go a long way toward normalizing your child's behavior in your own eyes, and giving them the freedom and security to know that they can do what they need to do without being judged, shamed, or punished. Instead of judging, see your children's quirky behaviors as their attempt to fit in here.

The typical response to behavior associated with autism—the toe walking, the flapping, and the stimming, is that it doesn't look right and it has to be stopped. I am inviting you to step away from that perspective and instead to ask why it's happening in the first place. As I suggested a moment ago, it's all about energy. It's all about a high-vibrational being, a child diagnosed with autism, experiencing that lightning bolt of energy and doing something physical in order to process that energy. Quite frankly, a nervous or angry parent just exacerbates the behavior, causing the child to toe walk, flap, spin, or stim even more. If you slow down your judgment, your child diagnosed with autism will slow down and more readily integrate that behavior. The reality of their level of functioning is what we are striving for while still being physically connected. This is the reality of "no time."

The challenge for parents of children diagnosed with autism is in understanding their children's awareness levels. These children will continue to reflect the emotions, thoughts, and conditioning that stand in the way of our functioning beyond time and space. And it's a very big challenge because their awareness is truly extraordinary by our standards. Take this example: Rebecca is a seven-year-old girl diagnosed with autism whose father was traveling overseas for his job. She could somehow sense when her father was walking into his hotel room after having completed a day of work. Rebecca would go to the front door of her own house and carry on a "conversation" with him about how her day went, and she'd ask him how his day was as well. Half a world and half a dozen time zones away, she knew when her father was done with work and walking through the door of his "home" in his hotel. How did she do that? She vibrates at a higher frequency than the rest of us!

That's why I call it Awesomism, because these are truly awesome children gifted with awesome abilities to perceive the world. I call it the oneness principle—the ability to be one with all things, to see across time and space. We go to meditation centers, ashrams, churches, synagogues, and mosques in order to get the slightest taste of what these awesome young children experience every minute of the day. One in 150 children today can be present in the physical sense on the planet and experience that sense of oneness and hold that level of energy—the way a typical toddler can hold a shovel and pail at the beach. As they become more accustomed to functioning here and as the collective consciousness rises in vibration, they'll be able to communicate more about that sense of oneness they experience, and the world will be a better place for it. It is the combination of reduced toxicity for better subtle-level function and increased awareness, thus consciousness and vibration of the collective, that will allow these children to be seen for who they are and what they offer to humanity.

Fear melts in the presence of understanding. So be aware of the magnificence of your children diagnosed with autism. Go beyond your physical perceptions and your emotional responses to their behavior. Move to an energetic understanding—an understanding of the energy they experience every day—and you'll get the full, delightful experience of who your child really is. There's nothing to fix! Instead, raise your own level of awareness, tune in to the higher level of awareness that your child experiences, and the behaviors that seem so frightening may well never disturb you again. There's always an explanation; the explanation is grounded in terms of energy and awareness, and your child simply needs your willingness to accept that his reality and yours may be very different ... and of course this is your unconditional love.[2]

---

2   For more information on right brain vs. left brain functioning in children diag-nosed with autism, please watch brain researcher Jill Bolte Taylor, PhD. at http://www.ted.com/talks/view/id/229; see also Taylor, My Stroke of Insight (New York: Viking Adult, 2006).

Chapter 6

Let's Get Practical

Throughout this book, I've been introducing a new way of thinking regarding how your child perceives the world and how you can perhaps better understand autism as it relates to your child. All this philosophy is terrific, you might be saying, but what do I do when my child begins to act out? What can I do at that exact moment to help my child?

In this chapter, I'd like to offer you some concrete steps that you can take in the heat of the moment, when your child needs you and you need a way to comfort him, and some fun things to try when life isn't so hectic. Before offering you these suggestions, I first want to give you one basic construct or organizing principle: You and I have been conditioned to function on the mental and physical level. First, we receive information by hearing or reading words. Next, we process the information, and finally we act on it. That is the mental level of functioning. We all understand physicality. We run, move, walk, and shake hands; we use our bodies in ways that are considered socially appropriate in our society. The first thing to realize when your child begins to act in a way that is not considered appropriate in our society, is to acknowledge that your child is not operating on a mental and physical level, but instead at a level of soul, pure feeling, or spirit vibration.

You've probably learned the hard way that words have almost no effect in these critical moments. Of course they don't, because your child is not vibrating on a mental level like yours. Your ability to change your feeling in the moment will make all the difference in the world. I'd like to share with you some approaches to reaching your child through the mastery of being present and making a clear observation of what is truly needed. The idea is to apply what we have discussed about their day-in day-out reality, so that you can bridge the gap from where they are to a place where they can function comfortably.

When your child becomes agitated for any reason known or unknown, it is helpful to first become still and watch, if only for a moment. A moment is all that it takes to turn the situation around. Become the observer, and there you will find it easier to calm yourself and reduce your emotional reaction. If you will do this first, any action that you take next will be significantly more successful. Another step that I have found to be consistently successful is to take your child's hand in yours, if they will allow, and press your thumbs gently into the palm of their hand. There is an energy vortex in the center of the palm and in the arch of the foot. Applying pressure to both of these points simultaneously has the wonderful effect of helping your child be more connected to his body in the very moment that you are trying to calm him. This also has the added effect of giving you a calming focus. The giving and receiving create the same relaxation. Remember that your child responds to the energy of a situation. You can see that if your child is already agitated, adding to the agitation will only make it worse. The good news is that because they are such amazing readers and mirrors of vibration, these children will change their behavior in the moment that you model a calm response. They will respond according to your moods and actions. If you are calm, they can be calm; if force is being used, they will respond with increased force.

As it happens, that's where we're going in the evolution of humanity. At some point, we are going to learn that war, force, brutality, and the whole "we had to destroy the village to save it" doesn't work. Instead, from a soul level, humanity eventually will learn to give people the tools they need in order to function. Okay, that's an aside, but I just wanted to relate what we're talking about to the bigger picture. Now let's get into practical things to do when your child is acting out.

At a vibrational or spirit level, any kind of force triggers a repulsion. It's basic physics. Too often adults get into a mindset of "I'm going to make you do it this way" or "You will do it this way" or "I'll physically force you or mentally coerce you to do it this way." As soon as you do that, children—not just children diagnosed with autism, but all children—will automatically go in a different direction. Children will do anything physically to get out of your grasp. What sets children diagnosed with autism apart is that you cannot talk them into a different type of behavior or feeling. You might be able to do that with a child not diagnosed with autism, at least some of the time. But with children diagnosed with autism—forget it. Force of any kind will never work with this population. The good news is that when you function at the level of calm presence, soul, and feeling, no coercion is needed. The following example may help.

While I was consulting in a self-contained classroom, Evan, a five-year-old boy who had just returned from a week's break from school, was demonstrating some significant frustration trying to follow the classroom routine. During circle time, he reached his threshold for overstimulation and began to act out. He was hitting himself and others, rocking and covering his ears. Taking a deep, cleansing breath I removed him from the group with physical assistance. He was agitated and did not want to go, but once he was taken just a couple of feet away (so he could not hurt himself or others), I removed any form of physical coercion, sat beside him and told him that I did not want to hurt him in any way. I could feel the energy shift with my statement to confirm his safety, and then I sat close and became the observer of his behavior.

He began to calm, as if by some magical force, and then reached over to me and took my hand to return to the group. I sat behind him in the circle but continued to just be the observer of his behavior, waiting to see what was needed next rather than trying to coerce him into what I thought he should do next. I let him lead, and that is just what he did. Evan took my hands and held them in his on either side of his head. He applied pressure and began to calm himself. This whole episode took about five minutes.

I have witnessed hundreds of these types of scenarios in various settings, and I can tell you that the outcome is always affected by the way the child is handled in the moment. Remember that because your child is responding to stimulation at physical, mental, emotional, and vibrational levels, most adults are never quite sure when the child will reach a saturation point. Because we cannot sense or know all that they take in during any given situation, it is almost always difficult to anticipate what will send them off behaviorally. For that reason, it is great to know that the only one you can truly manage in the situation is you. Now we can begin to see how it makes no sense to add negative energy to a child who is already overstimulated.

To bridge the gap between you and the child, be in the moment. This naturally takes you to the vibration of soul or spirit. If you're engaged fully with the child, it doesn't even matter what method you're using to connect.

What does it mean to be in the moment? First let's talk about what it means to be out of the moment. If you're worried about the future or reliving a moment in the past, you're not in the moment. If you're physically in the same place as your child but you are mentally a thousand miles away, thinking about anything from what you're going to make for dinner to what happened at work today, once again, you're not in the moment. What does it mean to be in the moment? In his book The Road Less Traveled, Scott Peck uses the term "cathexis" to describe a state in which a person and the object or person to which he is paying attention merge, becoming one. Peck gives the example of a person working in a rose garden. Time seems to stand still because the person is so utterly absorbed in what he or she is doing. That sense of connecting so deeply with a task at hand, or with a person in the room, is what Peck calls cathexis, and it's what I simply call being present in the moment. Children diagnosed with ASD live from the place of sensing their environment, so you can see that it would be important to practice being in the moment with your child at times when they are not agitated, so that in those heated moments you are able to replace agitation with calm.

Practicing comes very easily when we engage in activities with our children that naturally raise the vibration. When you engage in any creative endeavor, be it painting, dancing, singing, moving, or anything where you are totally present, you will have a relationship with your child unlike anything that could happen when you're sitting in front of a TV screen; yet even watching TV with your child can be an act of observation, an act of being present in the moment, if you so choose. In other words, what you're being is more important than what you're doing. Anything that your child and you enjoy doing together now are the situations where you are most likely to be fully present. Joy and presence seem to go hand in hand, so reflect on what those things are for you and use them.

To be in nature or participating in creative endeavors—singing, painting, dancing, and having fun—naturally raises the vibration and offers the potential to help you be very present with your child. These are great routine activities that can help you sense what it feels like to be connected to your child at a deep level. Again, it is not the act of producing a painting, completing a song, or taking a walk in nature that is what you are after. It is the feeling that you experience as you are engaged in that activity that is important. That sense of connection. Think about the adults in your child's life who are the most effective with him. Those are almost always the people who truly enjoy being with your child, the ones who are happy in their own lives and outlook on life and who assume your child can succeed because they see something beyond the label of autism.

Now let's get practical. What do you do when your child is acting out? Be there with the child. Minimize the use of words, and help them close down their sensory system for the time being. Remember their sensory systems are wide open all the time. These high-vibrational children are seeing, feeling, and hearing things on so many different levels that it is hard to process it all. You can help them to tone down the sensory input by turning yours down. This is especially true for young children who are under five and just learning how to operate their advanced sensory systems. Let's use their powerful ability to reflect your state to help them in these situations. I hear you asking, "How do I turn down my sensory system?" Let me give you an example and some suggestions.

There was a little girl in my office who was very visually sensitive. She would glance at every flicker of light from the window, saw things that were not physical in the room, and could not look at the office lights. She was also very active and was labeled ADHD. On this day she was running circles in my room and literally could not stop. First I took that deep cleansing breath to get in touch with me, and then I turned down the volume of my voice. In some cases that would have been enough, but because her primary heightened sense was sight, I had to take it a step further. I then turned down my visual input by closing my eyes. Within 30 seconds she was nose to nose with me and said, "It's OK. You can open your eyes." I opened one eye to see her sit down in front of me. So cute!

Knowing which sensory system is most heightened for your child or the one being activated in that moment can be the key to which one you want to shut down first, but consciously going through the steps of stopping movement, quieting your voice, covering your ears, and squinting or closing your eyes altogether is a basic model. This series of steps also can help you become more focused and present with the situation.

Rise to the occasion to make a real connection. These children are not in a place where they can absorb words, so you can't talk them into things. Instead, tell yourself what you'd like to see happen at this moment. Because we have mostly been trained to be left-brained thinkers and to use words to try and change a situation, we immediately and very naturally move into that mode during heightened tension. But children diagnosed with ASD are right-brain thinkers and only understand the words that you are saying in the heat of the moment, and that is only if they are able to match the emotion that you are feeling—which is a big IF.

If you are in the grocery store and your child is reacting to overstimulation, rather than pretending that everything is okay just for appearances, you would be much better off to model toning down your sensory system, and if that doesn't do the trick, tell him that you are frustrated with his behavior and then try to move him through the toning-down process. Your child is reading your emotions, and if your words and emotions do not go together, you will just get more confusion back. If, on the other hand, you have said to them, "I am frustrated," and they feel that same energy from you emotionally, they can relax. The two match, and that is one less thing that they have to process in the heat of the moment.

Now you can begin to see that we have been missing a very important step in working with these highly aware children. We have not been privy to how they operate and thus tried to use the mental/physical models. Sometimes those worked and sometimes they didn't, which made things even more confusing. But when they worked, it was because of how the person engaged with your child was feeling and not necessarily what they were doing. It is always amazing to me just how proficient children can be in their reflection, even when different people are involved in the same situation.

Here's an excellent example of the ability of these high-vibrational children to match the energy of another person, and it involves one of my greatest teachers, Sam. Sam, who was very verbal, had been diagnosed with OCD and was considered to have ADHD as well. He came to me one day to tell me about a dream that he had the night before. He said that in the dream there was a man who was trying to take energy away from other people. I asked him why the man was trying to do that. In his brilliance, he said because he doesn't know that he has everything that he needs, and so he thinks he has to take it from someone else. Of course, I was amazed by his clarity and wisdom and wanted him to tell the story to the teacher in the classroom. Mind you, Sam and I had had many discussions, and even at five years of age, he had always felt comfortable using words like energy and awareness with me; however, when he conveyed the story to the classroom teacher just minutes later, he completely changed the situation.

To her he said that he had a dream about Power Rangers, and the bad guys were trying to take power from the rangers. She asked why, and he said the bad guys didn't want them to have all the power and thought he could get it from them. I was amazed that this child was able to completely change the words of his story to reflect back the awareness of the listener. Verbal or nonverbal, through words or behavior, these gifted children do this all the time.

Let's get back to everyday situations. What other things can help your child be more effective and more comfortable in their daily routine? We all help our children in the ways we know to, usually based on what we think would help us. Your children feel your positive intention and absolutely do the best they can with what you are giving them, but they are high-vibration beings, and because most parents have not been educated in vibration as a way of being, they have been missing some of the pieces that are natural to their children. We know that color, music, and imagery have a certain vibration to them. Nature and all her elements also have a vibration that is familiar. This is why your children love art, learn best while listening to music, and are more likely to communicate when images are present to help them. It is why they are so connected to water and the other elements of earth as well as to animals. In these activities they are using their natural gifts of right-brained awareness and a vibrational view of the world to connect to what you would have them do. They are trying!

Something as simple as allowing your child to choose the color of shirt that they wear on a particular day can have a huge impact because, believe it or not, the child will choose the color or vibration that can support them for that day.   Remember the color scarves with Riley in chapter 1. He would choose the color of a large silk scarf to drape over us, and in the vibration of that color, he was able to make eye contact and answer my simple questions. From an energetic level, I watched him actually use the color to assist his awareness. The same was true with music. Riley would have me make different sounds or hum different notes. I once brought in tuning forks. He told me through gesture and response which sounds he liked, and he was able to be more present, and thus consciously aware of his environment, when he was hearing these sounds. We are already unconsciously doing this with our children when they learn skills through music and express themselves through art. Now it should be making more sense as to why they are successful with these strategies. Music therapy, equine therapy, and art therapy are all "therapeutic" because they are a vibrational match. They have elements to them that your child can use at his current level of high-vibrational function to make sense of this lower-vibrating world.

How much more effective would these same practices be if they were used with the conscious intention of helping our children? Now they can be! Here is a brief list of some of the ways that parents have used the vibration of color to help their children: One mother put colored sea salts in the bath to help ease her child's fear of bathing. Another let her child pick one of three different colored blankets to sleep with. One mom had different colored sunglasses for her child to choose, and another simply used her imagination and mind's eye to wrap her child in a soothing violet light as he slept, with the intention of soothing his system and giving him a good night's sleep. All reported success with these methods. Remember, because your child senses vibration first, working with energy, intention, and the focus of the mind's eye can be very effective. To many it would seem too subtle to make a difference, but to these children it can be "just what the doctor ordered."

There is so much more out there when it comes to helping your children be here fully with their gifts. They are teaching you as much as you are teaching them. You don't have to assume that you know the answer, or that you should know the answer, with regard to what helps your child. There's so much pressure on parents to know what's right. That's true for parents of all children, but with this population, that sense of "I ought to know how to take care of my own child" is particularly intense. Simply admitting that you don't know opens up all sorts of new possibilities. As you learn more, you feel more comfortable. And once again, the child reflects that to you. Parents of children diagnosed with autism can become almost fearful or in a constant state of anxiety regarding what will work or not work. I know the trial-and-error method is getting old, but now that you know about vibration and feeling your way through life, you and your child can partner in a place that feels comfortable to them. The more you feel your way through, the more sensitive you will be to your child's subtle levels of communication. You will begin over time to "hear" their guidance as I did Riley's. Your child knows just what will help them, and they can lead the way beautifully now that you have some of the basics.

Here is a beautiful example specific to your child's relationship to nature. Hannah was a lovely, petite, blond girl in a developmental preschool. She loved birds! She did puzzles of birds, made sounds of birds and carried around little toy birds from the classroom. She would throw an absolute fit if anyone took her birds from her. On this particular day, none of her bird friends were doing the trick for her, and she was very unhappy. The teacher and I decided to take the children outside a little early, as being outdoors always seemed to calm Hannah. Within 10 minutes, Hannah was over by herself in the corner of the playground with a beautiful hummingbird hovering right above her head. The teacher and I caught sight of it and watched spellbound. The other children on the playground stopped to watch as that hummingbird came right down between this little girl's outstretched hands at about her eye level and was suspended there for a timeless moment. If that is not an experience that brings one present, I'm not sure what is. Hannah was not obsessing on birds in the classroom; she was reflecting a powerful gift. Her ability to connect to this bird was what allowed everyone to be more connected on that day. She made it easy for us, but those amazing moments can be few and far between.

Does being present always work? Yes, but is being present in the moment always easy? Is feeling your way through easy? No! Our minds love to get in the way! It takes practice and awareness, and your children will give you plenty of that, one way or another. I have never met a parent of a child diagnosed with ASD who did not become naturally more aware, more attuned to their child and to the subtle nuances of an environment. Many of them did not know what was happening, and they would use other words to describe their transformation. The success rate of these children in bringing about subtle-level awareness for their parents and those that work with them is significant. It is also exactly the direction humanity is meant to go in … moving out of the mind and into the feeling, sensing, and knowing experience. When you truly move away from the mindset that focuses on the physical and mental levels and move into the spiritual/vibration and soul level, you can truly know that your child has Awesomism instead of autism. I am so grateful that consciously or unconsciously you have been traveling this road to higher awareness with your children. You have such an important role to play for all of us. As you learn these skills, so can all of humanity.

Chapter 7

Now … What About You?

So far we've focused on understanding the child diagnosed with autism, the traditional approach to autism, and the approach I've offered you based on understanding the energy and vibrational level of the child.

All well and good. But what about you? How are you handling the stress of this unexpected and most likely undesired situation? Whether you call it a gift, a blessing, or a curse, it's a lot for a parent to handle, especially if the situation is seen from the perspective of right or wrong based on a mental model of how children are "supposed to be." Physically, most children diagnosed with autism are drop-dead gorgeous. That actually can present even more of a dilemma for you, because you look at your child and say, "My child is so beautiful—how could this crazy thing be happening?"

Or they look "normal," and all of a sudden they start throwing an absolute fit in the grocery store. Or they can't interact on the playground with other children. You get a call from the kindergarten teacher saying, "Your child is not getting along with his classmates, and we need to put him in a different setting."

Or you're getting those disapproving looks from blue-haired old ladies in supermarkets, and maybe even comments like, "Don't you know how to control your child?"

And it's not always strangers who are making your life harder. You go to the doctor, and he says, "Okay, it's time for one more immunization." And you've got the nagging feeling that immunizations may be exacerbating the situation, despite whatever pharmaceutical industry-sponsored reports exist to the contrary.

Your mother says, "Oh, my God, my children never behaved like that."

Your spouse keeps saying, "His behavior's off, and I don't want to hear about this vibrational stuff. If he can't behave, I'm going to punish him."

Or your child goes on a play date, and the other parent says, "Your child can't sit still. She flips out anytime anybody else gets upset."

The well-meaning specialist says, "Your child should have reached all these developmental milestones by this period. Since they haven't, the likelihood is that your child is always going to need some kind of special educational services."

It sounds like a life sentence … or maybe even a death sentence. Your child is never ever going to change.

And there you are, trying to do the best you can for your child, trying to do what's right, feeling incredibly alone in the struggle, and all of a sudden you lose it. You start saying things like, "You know what? I don't want to have a kid diagnosed with autism. This has been a really crappy day. I don't want this challenge anymore."

And of course, after acknowledging your honest feelings—and who wouldn't feel that way?—the inevitable result is guilt for not wanting the child to be there, that way, in that moment. It doesn't mean you want your child to disappear. It just means that it's hard, you're lonely and sad, you feel frustrated, and you've had enough.

Every parent of a child diagnosed with autism whom I've ever met has felt exactly the same way on one level or another. It's tiring to have a child diagnosed with autism; there's no question about that. Children are exhausting anyway, but this just compounds the fatigue and frustration—because like most parents, you want to do the best you can for your children. And it's such a challenge. If you're going by the traditional medical model, or if you're just simply trying to "modify the behavior" of the child without really understanding him from a more intuitive level, people are actually better able to handle you. It's one thing to have a weird kid. It's another thing to have a weird kid with a weird parent, and that's suddenly the category that you're falling into in the minds of many people—and perhaps even your own mind.

Well, I'm here to tell you that you're not weird. What you are doing—what we're doing together—is trying to present to you, and to the world, a radically new way to approach the entire issue of what autism means and how to handle the awesome challenge of raising such a child, or perhaps you are raising more than one high-vibrational child.

There's nothing easy about your job. I want to acknowledge the courage that you have shown by opening your awareness by reading this book thus far and, if not outright accepting, then at least not immediately rejecting the approach I'm offering. So the question is this: What do you do when it seems that the whole world is against you in your quest to handle the needs of your child diagnosed with autism your way and not the traditional way? Obviously you've got to take care of yourself—because if you don't, who will? No one understands the strain you're under better than another parent similarly situated. So you can reach out to groups of parents of children diagnosed with autism, you can find other resources, you can take care of you to the best of your ability, and you can do whatever you want to make your life easier and more manageable. It's like what they tell us before we take off on a jet—put your own oxygen mask on first, and then put the mask on your child. In other words, if you're not getting oxygen, you can't really take care of anyone else. These external ways of supporting yourself are very important. From a vibrational vantage point, they take the edge off.

None of us is meant to go it alone, and if you are isolated, your personal resolve to do things in a new way can feel too much like a battle. Please know and remind yourself that you have a significant role to play in teaching others how to bridge the gap for your child, and armed with all the information, you can do just that. I truly believe that you have been gifted with these children because each of you have everything that you need within you to rise to the occasion. The ability to attract the support, care, and love that you need is within you, by simply setting your intention. So is the ability to connect and be with your child in a whole new way. You are co-journeying in a powerful way. Any activity that helps you to quiet the mind can help you with this connection. Meditation, yoga, walking, dancing, singing full out in the car … whatever it is …. use it!. It is so important that you feel connected to you!

Let me also suggest that instead of hiding your sadness, frustration, and anger from your child, that you communicate it to them in a matter of fact way: "Mommy is so frustrated right now." "I am feeling so sad and overwhelmed." " I get so angry that I don't know what you need." Make these statements about your own feelings versus placing blame or emotional energy on the child. Own your feelings and express them, and just watch what happens. Many say that children diagnosed with ASD do not understand emotion. I have seen that to be the furthest thing from the truth. What they don't understand is words and emotions that do not go together. When you say to your child "I am feeling frustrated" and that is just how you feel, the child fully understands emotion and in many cases becomes your greatest comfort. It is OK to allow your child to be your comfort in the moments that they can. You're not blaming your child for your frustration. It is not about them. It is about what you are feeling. As a side note, you will never teach this population about emotion by showing them a picture of it and naming the emotion. As there is not true emotion behind the picture, they have nothing to connect to.

The next suggestion I'd like to offer you is to move from a state of regret to a state of empowerment. In every one of the painful social interactions I outlined a moment ago, from the blue-haired lady in the grocery store to the comment from your physician, there is an element of shame involved if we buy into what other people are telling us how to feel. The basic message from the stranger in the grocery store, the impatient kindergarten teacher, the disapproving parent, or the unenlightened spouse comes down to this: "I'm right and you're wrong." Please hear me. Other people are not in charge of your emotional life unless you let them be. You are the only one in charge of the way you relate to your children. Please don't give those who don't have the whole picture the authority to make you feel bad! Don't give anyone that authority.

Let's back up a step and remember that none of these people understand what you now know about your children. None of them have been taught that your child feels, senses, and knows their way through life. The so-called "professionals" including most educators, physicians, and therapists have not been educated to understand the difference between your child's right-brain way of processing information and the world's left-brain dominance. Most of them have not had the day-in and day-out experience of being constantly "trained" in the subtle nuances of emotion, energy, and vibration, strictly by the trial-and-error process of trying to help their child manage a simple day. Up until a few short chapters ago, you yourself may have not even realized the scope of your child's abilities. All this time you have been receiving a crash course in how to function at a whole other level of being, and you had no idea that it was happening, nor did you have any rules for this game or language to explain it. This awareness will allow you to have compassion first and foremost for yourself and then for those well-meaning busybodies who think they have it all figured out. None of us get a road map with our children, but with these amazing high-vibrational beings, we not only have not had a road map, we weren't even in the same "state," metaphorically speaking, as they are.

Let's start with the grocery store, because the hissy fit in front of strangers is the most emblematic example of the situation that parents of children diagnosed with autism fear. I've got some interesting news for you: Pretty much all children throw tantrums in supermarkets, not just your kid. The elderly woman isn't singling you out because your child is diagnosed with autism, and you refuse to put her on drugs. You're tired and frustrated because you want to get your shopping done and get home. That's how the blue-haired lady feels. And that's how everyone in the store feels. In other words, it's not about the fact that your child is diagnosed with autism. It's about the fact that people sometimes have a very low tolerance for frustration, especially in a stressful situation like a shopping center in the late afternoon when everybody is tired, cranky, and hungry, and they just want to get out of the store and go home.

It doesn't take autism to trigger a child's explosion in a supermarket. All it takes is a fatigued parent and a tired kid. Mix in a few candy bars that the child has pocketed, add some parental disapproval, toss in a dash of the child's rebelliousness, and the fuse is lit. Where did autism fit into that scenario? It fits that the child diagnosed as ASD is reflecting the feeling of the whole. It's not about just being overtired, overstimulated, or over-sugared on a personal level. Very often in these situations, your child's sensory system is open to the energy of the whole store, all the people, all the frustration, and all the disapproval. They can walk around wide open all the time. Over time they learn bits and pieces on how to deal with the expansive awareness they are privy to, but no one has given them a course in how to handle their high-vibrational way of being either. Yes, the grocery store scenario could happen to any child at any time, and we both know that's true, but not to the same degree. So if that old lady is staring at you, you don't have to scrounge around for her approval by picking your kid up and yelling, "You're gonna do what I want you to do," or words to that effect. You might from time to time. All parents do. The best parents are not the ones who maintain perfect control of their emotions at all times, because short of Stepford Wives, there are no such people. Instead, the best parents are the ones who reflect on their own outbursts and say, "Man, that was not the way I wanted to handle that situation. I was so angry."

Wise parents review moments of where they were not their best selves with their children and determine, either on their own or in consultation with friends, parents, professionals, or other interested parties, a better way to handle the scenario. It serves nobody to say, "I've already screwed my kids up, so it doesn't even matter." A lot of parents will use that as an excuse not to say, "I'm sorry." Thinking that your child won't understand you or just being generally frustrated with the situation can give you a "reason" to jump right back on that treadmill of what you need to run to next, but instead of going there, take just a moment to say, "You know what? I screwed up. I've really messed up." Verbal or nonverbal, your child always will feel the sincerity of those words.

On your best of days, here are a few suggestions that will help any potentially overwhelming situation. You have already been taught by trial and error with your children no doubt that it is best to avoid more stimulation on an already overstimulating day, but your child does have to learn how to handle their sensory systems, so they can participate in life with you. When you do have to take them into a stimulating environment, make sure you talk to your child about how it feels in the store. Connect to your senses, be aware of what you are feeling, and articulate that to your child. Whether your child appears to be listening or not, he will feel the match of your words to the situation and will be calmed by that awareness. The more you stay in presence with your child and the more you stay out of the disapproving energy of others, the better chance both you and your child have of getting through the experience gracefully. Remember this is all based on energy/vibration. The energy of disapproval lowers your vibration and takes you out of connection with your child. Your ability to stay present with your child, increases the vibrational connection and naturally makes them more immune to the lower-vibrating energies of all the others around. Choose that high road as often as possible and feel the difference it brings.

So the remedy for the supermarket is this: Don't buy into the blue-haired lady's disapproval. But if that or something else triggers an explosive response in you, which you take out on your child, don't beat yourself up. It happens, and children are resilient enough not just to survive but to ignore parental outbursts, and remember with your child's "no-time, no-space" perception, they have no linear way to hold onto a negative situation and can let go of the experience long before you do. The key thing is this: Don't blame the incident on autism and autism alone. Any child in any supermarket at any time is a ticking bomb ... not just your kid.

Don't give yourself a hard time for not getting it right when you're out in public. You just have to let yourself make some mistakes, because the awareness that you gain from those mistakes is an awareness that we all will benefit from. When you're in private, you can raise your own vibration to get yourself in a place where you can truly commune with your child. You'll start noticing, "Oh, yeah, when I switch this behavior of mine, this works. Then when I do this, that works, too." Practice your new attitudes, approaches, and behaviors in private, surround yourself with others who are doing the same, and then go out into the world. You may see an important—and enormous—

difference in the way you respond to situations and in the way your child reacts to your responses.

Sometimes a parent's emotions are rooted in a desire to make the picture of his or her child look better to those around us. It's not your job. It's more beneficial all the way around to stay connected to yourself. Feel your emotions, express them honestly, and let them wash away to the best of your ability. The way your child looks is perfectly fine. In this moment and with that awareness, the next moment can look very different. You truly don't have to worry what other people think about you. This is a gift in and of itself. Moving out of the mind and the ideas of what something should look like and replacing them with the awareness that it is more important to allow the situation to just be what it is, is another skill that you are gaining through these interactions with your child. How many people go through their whole lives concerned simply by the appearance of things and never feeling or experiencing life? You, on the other hand, will naturally come to this place simply by virtue of the fact that at some point you just can't care about every old lady.

Parents ask me all the time what to say to those who openly display their disapproval. Remember they don't know what you now know, but on a very concrete level you could say, "My child experiences much more of the world than most do, and that can be a challenge at times." You can also say, "My child is reacting to the stress/energy of this situation, and you can help by taking your focus off of him." And if you have really just had enough and can't take it any more tell them, "My child is gifted at reflecting the negative energies/frustrations/stresses that people bring with them into these situations. Hopefully your day will get better, and then so will his." OK, now I will put my horns away, but I realize that sometimes it is just too much to take.

Now let's go to the teacher's office. The teacher says, "We're keeping your child in a self-contained classroom in kindergarten, because his behavior is not appropriate for a regular education classroom. He can't even go to the bathroom by himself yet. So he sure can't go to regular kindergarten class."

In the event that something like this happens, you don't have to accept the teacher's decision as the last word. If you cannot work out a solution with the teacher that you want, go over his or her head. Talk to the principal. Talk to the school therapist, if there is one. See what other resources are available in the community. But the bottom line is that you don't have to accept a negative verdict from a teacher, just because he or she is an authority figure. The reality is that if your child's teacher is reacting to your child's diagnosis of autism and its attendant behavior with a low-vibration response, it's time to move on and perhaps find a teacher and a classroom that operates at a higher vibrational level. These things are out there, and the more you command that your child be understood on all levels, the more that others will rise to the occasion and be more in harmony with what they have to offer your child and what your child can offer them. It might take a little bit of extra work and digging to find resources, but they are there, and your child deserves nothing less. Your focus now is on how the match between the teacher and your child feels. This is true of any professional but especially so for the teacher who will be with your child almost daily. Use your child's behaviors, words, and reactions as a reference guide as well. What the teacher does to help the child meet a goal is secondary to how they are doing it or, more importantly, how they are being with your child. The teacher may be strict, forceful, relaxed, or free flowing in approach. Any of these styles can work, but if the connection is not there, a successful experience will not happen.

As a side note, it is not realistic to think that a teacher will be on and connected to your child every day of the school year. We can't expect that of ourselves, and we can't expect it of them. I tell teachers all the time that if they have reached their saturation point, then it's time to take a walk around the school and regroup. I have frustrated more than a few teachers by taking that walk myself. But once they understand about vibration, they will know it is to everyone's benefit, especially the children's, to take the walk. When a teacher responds to this suggestion by saying that they can't possibly leave the classroom, I first ask if that is true. And if it is true, then I suggest that they reduce their sensory input, turn around, listen to their breath for a second, close their eyes if even for a moment, and try again. You could very nicely suggest the same to your child's teacher. Also know that schools are trying the best that they can to provide innovative approaches to working with your child, and some are doing so successfully, but many are still functioning from the physical/mental model. They will need your understanding of your child's various levels of awareness to help make schools a more appropriate place for your child.

What about the doctor who says that your child needs another immunization? Let's step back for a moment and think about the education of the typical doctor after leaving medical school. Do you know what the number one education provider for practicing physicians in our society happens to be? It's the pharmaceutical companies. They are the ones who provide pretty much all of the educational material that medical doctors in our society ever see once they have completed their formal education. Are drug companies motivated by the desire to help people? Sure. Is the profit motive at least as important to them? It would seem so. When a pharmaceutical company executive sees a school bus full of children going by, he's thinking, "What can I sell those kids?" Well, if they're healthy, what exactly can he sell them? Immunizations. Immunizing children is a multibillion-dollar business. States require immunizations, although you can have your child admitted to pretty much any school if you're willing to explain why you have chosen not to give your child any or all of the broad range of immunizations now required. In other words, you don't have to pump your kid full of junk just to be admitted to kindergarten, but the pharmaceutical companies aren't going to tell you that. Your doctor isn't going to tell you that, and most school nurses will not tell you that either.

Who makes money on immunizations? The pharmaceutical company ... and your doctor. Where does your doctor learn about the efficacy, safety, and possible risks of immunizations? From the pharmaceutical companies. It's a closed circle, and that circle becomes a bull's-eye painted onto the back of every young child in America. There is a place for traditional medicine, but that place, to my mind, is not at the tip of a needle injected into your child's arm over and over again. Is your personal doctor able to see beyond the "education" they receive? If so, they are probably willing to have an open discussion with you regarding immunizations. They are willing, at least, to discuss changing your child's immunization schedule and, at best, to give you resources on how to make an educated choice for your child. If you think that your doctor is too much in the grip of the "Big Pharma" mentality that makes billions of dollars by unquestioningly immunizing children before their systems are fully formed and able to resist the concoctions in those syringes, change doctors.

There is no law that says that your primary healthcare physician has to be a traditional physician who follows the medical model. Today, there is a wide range of homeopathic, holistic, and therapeutic experts who serve all children, not just children diagnosed with autism. Explore your options. If you feel that an aura of illegitimacy surrounds the practice of non-traditional Western medicine in our society, thank a physician. The American Medical Association and its sister organizations have done an outstanding job of making anyone who does not follow the traditional medical model look like a quack and a rip-off artist. Why? Because billions and billions of dollars are at stake, and so is the legitimacy of the traditional medical model. Take a look at other cultures and how they use alternative and traditional medicine together or use no traditional means at all. Also take a look at the statistics of autism in supposedly "less advanced" cultures compared to our own. Take a look at their immunization schedules too. What would happen if everyone in this country suddenly decided to eat well, get moderate exercise, get adequate rest, avoid unhealthy levels of stress, and work with their high-vibrational potential instead of against it. Traditional western doctors would starve in the street. Well, doctors are not about to let that happen. If you don't like your physician or his or her approach, once again, move on.

Don't accept a "life sentence" or a "death sentence" from anyone with regard to your child's future, because one day, between you and your child, the world is going to come to know a whole new way of being. Your child is going to be demonstrating things that the typical medical model cannot even fathom yet. We all have so much more to learn about the potential of these children, but from my vantage point our future looks very bright simply because they are here. While the medical community is waiting for things to be proved, you can already be experiencing the gifts that are inherent in your child. Do not buy into what I call "allopathic predeterminism." Allopathic simply means the traditional medical model, and predeterminism means that your child's fate is sealed even before he has a chance to find out who he really is. Twenty years ago, the attitude of doctors was to put these kids in an institution or in therapy for the rest of their lives, or get them a good job at the grocery store, bagging or shelving. That's because back then, nobody had this kind of information that says as your vibration increases, your child can feel more comfortable at home, and as that awareness spreads, they can feel more comfortable other places, and as the vibration of the planet increases, it means they can fully be present here and show us their gifts. And as they show us their gifts, there are many levels of self-expression that can unfold. These equate into jobs that we don't even know exist right now and new ways to do things that have been unsuccessful before.

Don't buy into predeterminism, whether it is thrust upon you by your doctor or your school system. They think your child has a disorder. We know your child has a gift. Don't let anyone say to your child, "Okay, I see all these things wrong with you. So I guess this is all you'll be able to do in life." Instead, only expose your child to teachers, healthcare professionals, and other helper figures who say, "I see all these things right with you, so let's see what the potential is." Let's be blunt: Don't let anybody tell you that your child is doomed to be in special education for the rest of their life, unless, of course, that special education is as special as they are. You have two tasks right now. One is to reduce the level of toxicity in your child's highly refined system so that it is as easy as possible for them to function here in the vibration where they currently find themselves. The other is to apply the principles of energy awareness that you have gained here to see the whole picture of your child. You have to get beyond the physical and mental to see the gifts inherent in this population, but once you do, there will be no stopping you in your connection to your child and your ability to be a true advocate for them.

Okay now, what about your parents? Parents of children diagnosed with autism do hear things like, "My children were never like that. You weren't like that as a child." Or, "You're not disciplining them correctly. If you would discipline them correctly, then they wouldn't be like this." Sometimes well-meaning grandparents of children diagnosed with autism put all kinds of terrible pressure on their adult children in this manner. I understand that this can be a huge source of stress for you, and I empathize. Some grandparents, however, have a natural tendency to be distanced enough from the diagnosis of autism, and all of the day-to-day responsibilities that it poses for parents, to be able just to see the brilliance of the child instead. They are more often observers instead of people who are coming from the position of, "How do we get these behaviors to go away? How do we get these kids to talk?" If you choose to let anyone in your family blame you for "what's gone wrong" with your child, your vibration can plummet you into depression. This happens all too often, and that's another reason why you can feel so isolated and inundated. It's the reason why you can get to the place where you say, "I just don't want to have this kind of child anymore."

Did you know that all different emotions have an energy level or vibrational frequency? In his book Power versus Force, David R. Hawkins, MD, PhD, gives a list of these. All research based, he lists shame at the bottom, with an energy level of 20, and peace at the other end of the spectrum at 600. These are the kinds of signs that your child is reading all the time. Guilt falls at 30, acceptance at 300. Your willingness to read new information and be open is at 310. Now you can really see that doing the best for you and doing the best for your child are the same thing. Your parents can be the trickiest ones of the bunch. Their comments can pack quite a punch, bringing up old wounds and fears. Practice telling them what would help you, and if they simply cannot be part of your support system, honor that.

Another very difficult situation can arise within the home itself. The experiences that you have with your child, especially as you connect at higher vibrational level, have the potential to alter all aspects of your life for the better. These experiences can either pull couples apart or bind them together at a level that is beyond what they have ever experienced before, but either way the movement into a greater level of consciousness is what is being offered. We already mentioned the spouse who thinks, "It's my way or the highway." Sometimes other siblings are involved, saying things like, "You give Johnny more attention." What those immediate family members are really saying is, "Hey, I'm here. Look at me! Pay attention to me! I've done this, this, and this. This is what I did at work today, or I made these kinds of grades at school, or I have this kind of athletic ability, or I made this other achievement, and you completely missed it because you were driving Tommy to therapy."

Well, the typical response of the parent in a situation like this is to go inside, to shut down, and to swim in the sea of guilt or frustration. But you don't have to come from a place of guilt. Instead, recognize yourself for what you really are: a great visionary, a great discoverer of truth, a student of higher vibration. All of the great explorers were criticized or perhaps even laughed at by their peers. "Oh, come on, Christopher Columbus, you know the world is flat."

Well, you know the world isn't flat. Anybody who goes down the road of discovery just a little bit opens the opportunity for everybody else to do the same thing. As you understand these principals and grow with them, so can your children and even your spouse. I understand that not everyone in your family is going to "get it." So your response can be an opportunity for education. When the doctor says, "Okay, we're going to give them round fifteen of immunizations," you get to say, "No, I'm sorry, we're not going to do that. And the reason we're not going to do that is…," and then you give your reasons.

Or you patiently explain to your non-autistic child that Tommy just needs a little more attention and care. You explain to them what he can do and what he has to teach. You share with them how they can help, and you accept when, just like you, they don't feel like helping any more. You don't love your other kids any less; this is simply the path and gift that you have all been given. It is always a choice of how we see things, and children can get that faster than most adults. Don't underestimate your other children. They have a unique connection to their siblings, and even though they may bemoan the situation, they often have insights that are invaluable. They are already good at being present, they still know about joy, and they are usually fabulous observers. Within your home, siblings of children diagnosed with autism can be your greatest resource. They are usually one step closer to where you, as an adult, are trying to get. You're going to have to educate your other children, but never underestimate them. Let them help you through this process. Ask them what they notice and what they think about various situations that you find yourself in.

Educating your doctors and your general-education teachers is another ball game. Find out what their level of awareness is, and then take it from there. I had one client who told me that she started every "education" session with "This may sound totally weird, but Johnny is able to … or knows … or feels …" Then she just sat silently until they asked a question. Brilliant! Special education teachers can be a little bit better about "allowing" this sort of discussion as many of them, by virtue of their training are not as vested in the traditional modes of education.

The overall shift that you're making is from shame to empowerment. You no longer have to feel bound, burdened, and limited by other people's belief systems, profit motives, or hidebound attitudes of "This is the way we've always done it." What will happen, if you are willing to demonstrate the courage that it takes—and it does take courage—to stand up to all of these authority figures, relatives, and blue-haired ladies in the supermarket, is that you will create a vibrational environment that's more conducive for your child diagnosed with autism. And guess what? All of a sudden your child will start acting better, looking better, and generally be more connected the way you probably wish him to be. But it has more to do with the vibration you're establishing than with anything else.

If your spouse isn't onboard with you, you've got to stick to your guns. Typically, if both parents are still in the situation to begin with, it's my experience that they both really do want what's best for the child. It's just that one may understand it in a slightly different way from the other. Perhaps your spouse wants to do things in a more traditional way, but only because he's so uncomfortable with the entire situation. If you can model something else, at some point your spouse may just get onboard. If you spouse doesn't want to do so and wants to stay at that lower vibration, then the relationship may not work. It's not about applying brute force in your marriage, in the doctor's office, or in school. Instead, it's about making choices based on who the child is rather than on what's socially comfortable and acceptable for everyone around you. It's not about appearances. It's about doing what best supports your child. And in so doing, not only will you be giving your child the best possible shot at life, but you'll be dramatically enhancing your own life as well. Who cares for the caregiver? You. It's your job—it's your responsibility—to take care of yourself. In so doing, you will establish the vibration that will make it possible for you to take care of your child diagnosed with autism in a way that will give him or her the best life expression possible, and that's what all of our work together is truly all about.

Chapter 8

Treating Autism with Pharmaceuticals

One of the standard approaches for treating the diagnosis of autism in our society is, of course, pharmaceuticals. There are two basic categories of parents who give drugs to their children diagnosed with autism. One group is parents who trust their doctor and come from the traditional belief, which the pharmaceutical industry spends billions of dollars to reinforce, that medicine makes you healthy. And then there are other parents who are uneasy about giving drugs to their children diagnosed with autism, but they don't know of any alternative. In this chapter, I want to share with you my thoughts about treating the diagnosis of autism with drugs. As you can imagine, it's is far from my first choice. If you come from the traditional medical model that says, "Trust the doctor," by the end of this chapter, I hope that you will reconsider your position. And if you are among the parents who are uneasy about treating autism with drugs, I hope this chapter will give you the confidence necessary to find another way.

I define children diagnosed with autism, as we have discussed at length, as individuals who operate at a higher vibrational level than the rest of us, and I see them as harbingers of a new era in the world, when we will all operate at a higher energetic level. The behaviors associated with the diagnosis of autism trigger fear in parents, because their children don't "look like" the rest of us and act, or act out, in ways that are often socially unacceptable—in the classroom, in the supermarket, in the home. Sometimes parents want to use pharmaceuticals to help their children behave in a more normal manner.

Pharmaceuticals don't provide recovery from autism, because autism is not an illness. They could actually be compounding the issue by adding toxicity to the body. The best that pharmaceuticals can hope to do is temporarily modify the behavior of these children. But as any physician will tell you, anything strong enough to help you is strong enough to hurt you as well. Then the major problem with putting pharmaceuticals into these highly delicate systems is that they throw these children's systems into states of havoc. This is why parents continually find themselves needing to readjust, and usually upwards, the dosage of any given drug they give their children. Or they switch from one drug to another. It stands to reason that the tampering with the biochemistry of any individual, especially the delicate system of a young child, will lead to unacceptable and undesirable biochemical changes. Yes, the behavior might be alleviated for a short period of time. But the behaviors the drugs are meant to prevent can recur as the child's system develops a tolerance for the drug, and the child's biochemistry has been altered as a result. Even more important than all of this is the awareness that the added toxicity in your children creates certain behaviors that make it more difficult for you and your child to see the Awesomism. If you work to decrease the toxicity, that will naturally decrease behaviors, increase connection, and increase the display of Awesomism versus autism symptoms.

Does this mean that there is no place in the world at all for pharmaceuticals in the treating of the diagnosis of autism? I wouldn't go that far. If your child is currently on medication, I beg of you not to stop the drugs cold turkey. That could cause even more damage. Nobody goes from pharmaceuticals to vibrational energy overnight. On top of that, if pharmaceuticals will alleviate some of the negative energy thrown at your child day in and day out in school, by other family members, or from any source, then go ahead and continue the drugs until you find a healthier alternative, which we'll discuss later in this chapter. But don't stop there. If you do stop there, you are creating a huge problem for yourself and for your child down the road.

Go ahead and use the drugs for now, and get a little bit of physical relief. But once you have that physical relief, use it to look at some of the different issues and the different layers of the diagnosis of autism that we've discussed in this book. If you don't, your child will most likely end up staying on pharmaceuticals for a long time. And yes, your child may look like the rest of us and act like the rest of us in the short term, but that same child diagnosed with autism is not necessarily going to bring her full gifts to the planet, because the drugs inevitably shut these children off from the full realm of the spirit with which they have been endowed. It is interesting that at a time in history when the vibration of our children and the planet is increasing, there is also a significant increase in the use of pharmaceuticals that cause chaos to those systems.

The specific purpose of pharmaceuticals in the treatment of the diagnosis of autism is to assist with concentration. These drugs are intended to alleviate behaviors and reduce agitation. They're supposed to help children focus. Do they work? It depends on whom you ask. From my vantage point, these drugs are actually counterproductive, because, as I said, they deaden the child's energy and keep her from being her true and best self. They do have a certain efficacy— otherwise, perhaps, no one would use them. The marketing ability of big pharmaceutical companies can only go so far, after all. Teachers will tell me that they can tell when children have changed their medications. Or some parents and teachers will say that they can tell if a child hasn't taken his medication. But again, it's a matter of perception. When I look energetically at the same child and he has pharmaceuticals running through his veins, what I see is a deadening of his vibrational frequency. And when you deaden the vibrational frequency, then you also deaden the ability to be connected to everything. The gift of autism is the ability to feel connected to everything; losing that ability, that interconnectedness with the world around them, actually reinforces a sense of separateness that leaves the child feeling lonelier than ever. That's how I view it.

Even if a drug is successful—if success is measured by limiting the behaviors that some parents, doctors, teachers, and other professionals wish to reduce—a drug is still a drug. There is a natural tendency within the body to find balance, which means that a body seeks to balance anything injected into it. Call it homeostasis, call it finding balance, or simply call it developing a tolerance, but eventually, all of a sudden, that drug isn't going to work anymore. And now the child will have to receive another drug. And then another drug. And that young, small body must struggle to find balance with all these pharmaceutical insults to the system. What's going on with the behaviors as the body finds that sense of balance? All the behaviors that the parent hoped to prevent through the drugs come right back. The pharmaceutical companies will be the first to tell you that after you've used a drug for a certain period of time, it won't work anymore, so you'll have to use another one. The result in the child's body: chaos. The result in the child's behavior: despite all that biochemical damage, all the behaviors are back.

Pharmaceuticals for the treatment of autism are similar to pharmaceuticals used to treat mental illness and depression: You only know if you gave the patient the right dose by monitoring the behavior. There's no exact science to it. A child may get better, and that tells you that the child received the "right" dose. Or the child doesn't change, so the dose or the medication wasn't correct, and you've got to either up the dosage or try another drug. And all this is done not in the name of curing or changing autism, but instead just to manage behaviors or help the child be focused enough to learn. Is it worth it? Maybe instead of putting a bandaid on the issue of their behaviors, we need to understand them first and find ways to help them work with the amazing gifts they have been given.

Why do so many parents have a comfort level with pharmaceuticals? Because they, and their children, experience relief. A quick fix, parents often say, is better than nothing. The problem with quick fixes is that they don't last long. I can put a wire around my muffler and hold it up that way, rig it to make it work so that my car can keep going, but sooner or later, that muffler is going to fall off. That's because it was just rigged to stay together for a while, but I hadn't really dealt with the issue. It's going to get louder and louder, and finally the wire is going to break and the bolts are going to fall off, and it's going to drop off on the highway somewhere. That's not a solution—it's a temporary fix. I see pharmaceuticals in the same way.

There's a tragic irony in all of this. One of the main culprits in the explosion in the number of diagnoses of autism in recent years is the number and frequency of the vaccinations children are now required by law to receive. I'm aware that recent studies have denied this implication. I'm not buying the argument, however, that vaccinations have no negative side effects on our children. You don't need to be a Harvard-trained molecular biologist to understand the concept of "garbage in, garbage out." If you put enough stuff into a little kid, you're going to end up with a different kind of biochemistry in that child's body. Your high-vibrational child will feel the effects of that disturbance as it moves out through all vibrational levels of their system because they are aware, to one degree or another, of all of those levels, from the densest physical body to the spiritual or energetic level.

This isn't Left Coast vibrational thinking; this is common sense. Big Pharma is making a fortune through immunizations. Turning children into pincushions is an extraordinarily lucrative business opportunity for them. And then they get a second opportunity to make another fortune … by providing the drugs to treat the diagnosis of autism, which is itself a function of the vaccinations these children were given. Big Pharma collects while they are making a mess of your child's highly refined system, and Big Pharma makes money while they are cleaning up that mess. But they are not really cleaning it up. When looking through the eyes of vibration, the place where your children function naturally, they're only making it worse. Does that mean that, down the road, they will derive a third windfall by creating medication to alleviate the damage that they have caused to the biochemistry of our children? Stay tuned. The fact of the matter is, if we keep changing a child's biochemistry, by layering in one drug on top of another, or increasing the dosage, we're constantly keeping these children in a state of chaos, and that's what we were supposed to be trying to get them out of by giving them those drugs.

Do I believe that Big Pharma is acting maliciously to harm children in order to make a buck? I wouldn't go that far. I'm not that much of a conspiracy theorist, even on my worst days. I truly believe that everyone is always doing the best they can with the information they have and the interest they hold. But I do find it painful to see just how addictive our society is to the medical model, which says that drugs make things better, even when the anecdotal evidence is abundant that drugs make things worse.

The social pressure on parents to immunize their children is enormous. I have four children of my own, and by the forth, I had enough information to make the decision not to immunize. Nurses have said flat out, "I've got to tell you that I think you're completely endangering your children by not having them immunized." So I have to be able to marshal my confidence and respond, "I have to tell you that I feel the opposite way, that I would completely endanger my children by giving them immunizations. So we are just going to have to agree to disagree." My method is not for everyone, but delve into the literature and find out for yourself. Parents who study the literature surrounding the damage that immunizations can do to their children must be ready to stick to their guns and tell family physicians, preschool and kindergarten teachers, daycare center operators, and anyone else, over and over again, "I have a rational set of reasons for not immunizing or not fully immunizing my child." It may not be easy to stand up to that social pressure, but it is urgent that you do so to protect your child. Similarly, standing up to a family physician who insists on treating with drugs a child diagnosed with autism isn't easy either. But you don't have to go down that path. We've talked throughout this book about the importance of recognizing the higher vibrational level of these children. Meeting them where they are, instead of forcing drugs upon them, is the best way to ensure the integrity of their body chemistry.

You can't mess with body chemistry without changing the way a child perceives the world. Take a look at what's going on with drugs for ADD and ADHD. A body of evidence is emerging to the effect that these drugs are causing great depression in kids later on. Some of the young people who have committed acts of atrocity by shooting up their schools are children who have been given these pharmaceuticals throughout their lives. What will be the effect of autism drugs over the long term on these children? What will their biochemistry look like ten or twenty years from now? It's impossible to say with certainty, simply because the only way you can know for sure is to have a large enough sample of individuals who have ingested these drugs and then are observed over a long period of time. The reality is that the "beta testers" for these drugs are not lab rats or mice. The beta testers are your children. It is simply impossible for a drug company to know what the long-term effect of a drug will be until the long term unfolds. I don't care how much short-term relief is possible for parents of children diagnosed with autism; I would not want my child to be a guinea pig for the pharmaceutical industry, and I'm sure you feel the same way.

So what are some approaches you can take?

- If your child is currently taking pharmaceuticals as a treatment for autism, you can choose to wean your child off those drugs in a safe manner. Work with your physician to do so, or find another more holistically minded physician who can help you.

- Explore the world of alternative medication. There are countless wonderful alternative medical practitioners who have great experience and success with children diagnosed with autism. Ask around in your community and go online to find the naturopathic or homeopathic health practitioners, energy workers, acupuncturists, and others who can provide alternative ways of treating the condition. There is so much out there. How do you tell who's real from who's a fake? Your instincts won't let you down. The nice thing is that now so many MDs are getting frustrated with the limitations of their own training and are being educated in these alternative specialties. It's very easy these days to find someone who has an MD and yet is providing alternative approaches.

- Consider the diet that you are feeding your child. White flour and white sugar are toxins for all of us, and they are especially dangerous for the delicate biochemistry of a child diagnosed with autism. White flours and white sugars are allergens in the body, and you're trying to reduce the allergens and toxicity in the body.

- Explore vibrational medicine more deeply. Find a practitioner in your community who can help you understand and work with the energetic pattern of your child, because the characteristics of autism, like the behaviors that so concern parents, are bound to shift as well.

Above all, recognize that just because the doctor wears a white lab coat and sits in an office surrounded by degrees, he or she is not the ultimate first choice health practitioner for your child. David R. Hawkins, MD, PhD, lists responsibility at the opposite end of the energy level spectrum from guilt. We can't give the responsibility of our children's well-being over to anyone without asking a few questions. If you are satisfied with the answer, go with that, and if what you are being told doesn't add up, seek your answer somewhere else. Just like your children, the more you "see" the more potential options you have.

Chapter 9

Next Steps

In this chapter, I'd like to share with you some thoughts about how to find the best possible resources and information for you and your child diagnosed with autism. I'm actually going to send you on a wild adventure, careening around the Internet, your public library, and your neighborhood, in search of the latest and the greatest ideas about helping your child be all he or she can be. But before I do that, I'd like to take a moment and emphasize the word "be."

So before we talk about what to do next, let's talk about what matters even more—the question of being.

In a society where we are consumed with doing more, accumulating more, and racing from one time-compressed activity to the next, whether it's at work or at home, we have lost the art of quieting the internal chatter and being with ourselves, our children, our spouses, and with the world. We're all in such a frenzy these days that ultimately we are sprinting on a mad dash further away from our true selves.

If the modern, Western way of life is all about doing, the Eastern, traditional, Zen way of life, if you will, is all about being. Today, there's more of an emphasis on the idea of being as opposed to doing than ever before. Author and speaker Eckhart Tolle and others are making the term "being in the moment" commonplace. But it's still a drop in the bucket compared with the oceanic pull toward going and going and going. We've turned into a race of Energizer bunnies, but in our headlong race to cross items off our task lists, we are losing sight of the most important thing in life—who we really are.

Compare the typical American frenetic approach to life with the startlingly different approach to life of the child diagnosed with autism. If we are purely about doing, which is all too often the case, they are purely about being. They are pure reflectors and realtors to spirit, pure energy, pure vibration, and they are reminders to us that there's more to life than the piling up of trophies that our consumerist culture is all about.

We are primarily material in our approach to life; they're primarily spiritual. We have feet of clay; they seem to live in the clouds. We function from a dominate left hemisphere, and they seem to function from a dominate right.

One thing this book does not offer is a seven-step program toward "treating" or "resolving" or "overcoming" your child's diagnosis of autism. There really is no such thing as a cookie-cutter, one-size-fits-all approach, because for all their similarities, these wonderful children are as different from each other as are snowflakes descending from the heavens on a winter day; and although there are some common gifts among them at a vibrational level, I have seen they can have very specific "jobs." There are, however, some general measures that will help point you in the right direction. At a physical/mental level these are as follows: Clean up the level of toxicity in your child's body by reducing the types and amounts of pharmaceuticals that you give your child; these include vaccinations and drugs. Clean up your child's diet, especially as it relates to stimulants such as processed sugars and foods and other toxic substances. Reduce your child's exposure to toxic materials and products. This process allows you to see the gifts of Awesomism versus the characteristics of autism.

At a soul/spirit level these measures are advised: Increase the vibration of your interactions with your child by participating in more creative, fun, connective time together; this includes dancing, singing, movement, drawing, etc. Spend more time in nature and/or with animals, and practice being versus doing. When you have begun this process, pay attention to the way in which you are being led and the ways in which your children are confirming your direction. Everything is so much easier to experience at the level of vibration. As I have said before, the more consciously aware you become, the more potential there will be for a powerful expression of your true self. That is where the magic happens. If I were to offer seven steps to solving your perceived problem, I'd be lying to you, because as we have discussed repeatedly, I don't see autism as a problem. I see it as a gift to individual families and a gift to the world. There are ways to expose the Awesomism in autism, and that is all that I have to offer.

If these children are all about being, then the solution must be rooted not in doing but also in being—in being with them and, just as importantly, in being with ourselves. Certainly there is much to do if one is the parent of a child diagnosed with autism. There are meetings with teachers, healthcare providers, and other experts. There is information—and misinformation—to be sorted through. There are conversations with immediate family members, parents and grandparents, neighbors, parents of other children, and of course that ubiquitous blue-haired lady in the supermarket that must take place. So don't get me wrong—there's nothing necessarily easy about raising a child diagnosed with autism, especially when most people are trying to get them to fit into the old mold. You have responsibilities, burdens, challenges, and difficulties that other parents could never even imagine.

At the same time, you have an opportunity, an invitation to explore your own relationship to yourself. Are you running from yourself? Are you hiding from yourself, burying yourself under an endless pile of activities, responsibilities, and tasks? Do you ever take time for yourself? It's hard to do so, especially in a world that seems to be speeding faster and faster. But do you? The most important relationship we have is not with our spouses or our children but with ourselves. If we cannot be comfortable with ourselves, how could we possibly be comfortable with anyone else? If we cannot give ourselves the love, nurturing, time, and patience that we need, we cannot do the same for others. Nor can we expect others to provide us with the time and presence that we must give ourselves. It's not their job! Their job is to have the best possible relationship with themselves!

The best interpersonal relationships—whether they are spouse-spouse, parent-child, friend-friend, or other—all take place when both parties are coming from a place of comfort in terms of being themselves. This is where honesty lives. This is where integrity lives. This is where courage lives. When we meet on a being-to-being level, there's nothing to explain, nothing to demand, nothing to expect, nothing to forgive. This is where we can truly be with ourselves. And this is where we can connect with our children diagnosed with autism.

We train our children in the currency of time from an impossibly early age. Five-year-olds can find their peaceful lives transformed into a not-so-fun game of beat the clock every morning as they try to make the school bus for kindergarten. They see their parents rushing around feverishly, and they assume that this is the proper way to approach life. Without thinking, and without intending to do so, we unconsciously condemn our children to the same treadmill of frenetic and all too often meaningless activity on which we find ourselves. We can do that to a child who does not have the diagnosis of autism, because unfortunately, they can be trained to become little adults, racing joylessly from one activity to the next, distracting themselves with technology, not knowing what it's like to have a relationship with themselves. The hardest thing in the world with a child is to take away his or her GameBoy! Everything else, from getting them to the dentist to getting them to eat their spinach, is radically easier than trying to pry that toy from their hands. In other words, so-called normal kids are adrift in the world of doing and doing and doing still more.

And then here comes the child diagnosed with autism, the essence of pure being, who knows nothing of and couldn't care less about your compulsion to keep doing and doing and doing. They just don't get it. They never will. They cannot be narcotized into understanding the world of doing. They cannot be "behavior modified" into trading being for doing. It's just not going to happen. It's just not who they are. So when I talk about the responsibility of the parent to create an energetic match between herself or himself and the child diagnosed with autism, what I'm really talking about is transcending the compulsion to do and instead meeting that child on the field of being.

Sounds vague, you say. What exactly is the realm of being? In the realm of being, we are simply aware of what is up for us. We are aware of what the mind is telling us and the feelings that evokes. It's being connected to our inner world and all the grace that offers versus being totally focused on the outer world. It's hard to just sit there without the TV on, without the compulsive reach for the PDA to check our e-mail, without making a mental list of a thousand things to do later, or without ruminating on what we should have done, what we should have said, what he shouldn't have said, what she might have said, what could have been, and so on. In other words, we adults spend most of our time rethinking the past or thinking about the future—what we need to do, what we should have done, what we'll get next, what we might lose, what we did lose, housing prices, gas prices, everything.

Okay. Now toss all of that mental trash out of your head and just sit there and be. Go on, I dare you.

If you can stay in the moment, if you can resist that temptation to do something or make a list about what you need to do or think about what you should have done, then wow! That's awesome! If you could do it all day long, you'd have to call it Awesomism. Guess what? That's the gift that your child possesses. That's the skill or ability or mindset or mental structure that your child diagnosed with autism possesses. So instead of trying to shape that child to look like us, what we really ought to be doing—there's that word again, doing—is studying our child and his ability to be in the moment, to truly be in the present moment without recourse to the past or the future—and just experience time for what it is—a miraculous sense of presence, of being here now, as they used to say in the sixties. That's who your child with autism is. He's a "be here now" kind of being. And he, without thinking, does a fabulous job of reflecting back to not only you but all of humanity the various behaviors and emotions that stand in our way from accessing all that the moment offers. He has no expectations of you at all. But he will be most comfortable—and thus feel less of a need to act in the compulsive and often disturbing ways that children diagnosed with autism so frequently display—if you'll stop doing and start being. Get out of the past and get out of the future and get into the present moment, because that's not just where you'll find yourself. It's where you'll find your child. Waiting for you. And delighted that you've made the decision to join him there. It is where you will be open to the full scope of what is possible in the moment. It is where you will see beyond what is physical and mental in nature. It is where you will connect not only with the brilliance of your child but with the inner connectedness of all.

So you don't need seven steps. You don't need a ten-week program. You just need to sit for a moment and be. Because that's what your child is all about—just sitting and being. Or running and being or flapping and being or repeating phrases over and over again and being, but the commonality, the thread that ties together all of your child's activities and behaviors, comes back to this basic concept of being in the moment.

Is it really that simple? Yes, it is! Okay, you still feel the need to find the right professionals and explain things to the teacher and deal with the blue-haired lady in the supermarket, but as you bring this state of being into all that you do, that is where the real joy is. There are many things that you feel you must do as a parent of a child diagnosed with autism—there's no question about that. And yes, you seem to have more responsibilities with your child diagnosed with autism than you may have with your other children, or more than other parents may have with their children who do not have that diagnosis. But on the other hand, those other parents don't have a role model to remind them that being is where it's at, and that doing and having are secondary in life. Letting go of the need to make these children look just like us, brings the real work into focus (the work of connecting unconditionally), and then development unfolds naturally.

So that's why there is no seven-step program, no ninety-day plan, no worksheet, no nothing. You don't need any of those things. You can grasp the essence of your child diagnosed with autism in a moment—in any moment in which you meet him at the level of being, because that's where they can be found. You don't have to have all the answers. You don't even have to have any of the answers. What you have to have is presence. In those moments, the answers come, not from some external authority, but from within you. They are there, and they have always been there. You have just been so busy that you forgot to look in the most obvious place. Be present with your child, watch him, sense him, without the words of those that disapprove running through your head. Overcome your fear. Forget about what the neighbors and the woman in the supermarket think. And if your doctor, schoolteacher, speech therapist, or other professional caregiver isn't on the same wavelength, get rid of that person and find someone more amenable to your way of thinking. They're out there, and when you are connected to yourself and your child, you will find them effortlessly. You will know what resonates with your child's well-being and what does not. The answers that you find may not be the ones you expect, but they will be ones you can trust.

And that brings us to the answer to the question posed at the beginning of this chapter—now what? It's time for you to go exploring. As an exercise, I'd like to invite you to type into your Internet search engine the phrase "alternative therapies for autism." You'll get so much stuff that it'll blow your mind, but that's okay. Just pick out ten Web sites, study them, and see if there's anything there that resonates with you. Believe me, you are not the only parent in America, or in the world, for that matter, distressed by the approaches to autism currently offered by the pharmaceutical manufacturers and by traditional MDs. You'll get all kinds of information. You might find the woman who is an autistic individual who's playing with water and explaining to people that she's in harmony with the water and communicating with the water and that as she moves the water and it moves with her, she's actually having a dialogue with the water. Okay, that might be a little out there for you, or it may lead you to a question. Try each of the next nine Web sites, and see what you find. There is no one-size-fits-all approach, but the more things you look at on the Web, the broader the range of approaches that you'll discover. And there's going to be something out there that makes sense for you. I am not trying to throw you to the wolves or expose you to experiences that are too uncomfortable. I simply want to demonstrate to you that you and your child have all the answers that you need. This little experiment can help you practice being so aware of how you feel about any suggestion, recommendation, or new method that you will feel empowered to make the best choice that you can for your child. It is only an exercise in feeling your way through. If what you choose stops being a match, you will know it and be empowered to choose again. I have my personal favorites related not just to autism but to all the topics we have discussed in this book. They are:

www.childrenofthenewearth.com This magazine has all kinds of articles on high-vibrational children and subjects related to them. It also has great resources.

www.jillboltetaylor.com She is a neuroanatomist who had a left-hemisphere stroke. Her ability to discuss the function of the right brain from a personal account is nothing short of brilliant and will give you a good sense of how your children might experience the world.

www.energymedicine.org This is the Web site of medical intuitive Laura Alden Kamm. Her information will speak for itself, but she is extremely gifted at seeing the inner working of the body. They call her a walking MRI.

www.intutiveteachings.com Jennifer Crews is gifted at helping parents develop their intuition and knowing the needs of their children.

www.eckharttolle.com If you haven't been introduced to him yet, Eckhart Tolle is the father of being in the present moment. His books, The Power of Now and The New Earth will point you in the right direction to being in the moment in all areas of your life.

www.whatsuponplanetearth.com Karen Bishop's Web site offers insight into the energetic shifts and symptoms that accompany the process of conscious human evolution.

www.abraham-hicks.com Ester Hicks is in my estimation the "Founding Mother" of the Law of Attraction. Her work with the vibration which is Abraham can assist you in better understanding your innate emotional guidance system. Also please check out Abraham's response to a questions on autism.

But please don't take my word for it, take them back to yourself and see if they feel right.

You can go on YouTube as well, and type in autism. A swarm of videos will present themselves for your consideration. Pick ten and see what you discover. You don't have to watch any video in its entirety. If it doesn't make sense, move on to the next one. The blessing of the Internet is that everyone has the ability to broadcast his or her experiences, knowledge, opinions, and emotions. The downside is that the material is unfiltered; there are no "experts" to tell you, "This makes sense, and this doesn't." But that's what my approach to autism is all about—the best expert in the world isn't wearing a white lab coat. It's you! And what qualifies you as an expert is your open-mindedness to consider approaches that others may scoff at, to look the traditional medical model in the eye and say, "I can't buy that lock, stock, and barrel," and to stand up for your child and your right to be with your child in the manner that makes the most sense to you.

I understand that the advice I'm giving here flies in the face of one of the basic facts about human nature—most people like to be led. People like experts, self-appointed or otherwise. I'm not denying my own experience or knowledge base with regard to the integration of the various levels on which your children function.. But I'm also not claiming a hammerlock on the truth. My desire is to give you back your empowerment in this situation and to show you what Riley showed me about your children. He helped me unlock my gift, and all the children that have followed have brought clarity, understanding, and resolve to what I know to be true. I believe that this gift of being able to connect to your children on the physical, mental, emotional and spiritual levels of their being and to understand their high-vibrational vantage point was given to me so that I could bring them closer to you. I know that this ability is for you to possess as well and that by being with your children day in and day out, you are well on your way to that experience. If you need a little assistance on the way, I would be honored to help you more personally understand the energy system of your child and support you in the use of your intuition to carve a path for you and your child. I can help you become more empowered through your communication with and about your child. I can point you in the direction of what you think you lost when your child received the diagnosis of autism, helping you find your personal way to Awesomism. I can tell you what I see and sense vibrationally, while I help you to develop that same skill until you are confident to do it on your own. I truly am grateful that you and your children are here at this crucial time in human evolution. I am grateful that you are open to something new, and I am grateful to be a part of this journey with you. Your children truly are awesome.

What I've been trying to provide you throughout this book is a new way of thinking about the diagnosis of autism so that you can step away from traditional approaches which all too often can do more harm than good. There was a loss here—you no longer have the "expert" or guru telling you what you must do. You've got to sort things out for yourself. When you go on YouTube, you'll find a medical doctor who says that there's no correlation between immunizations and the diagnosis of autism. On the next video, you'll see a homeopath who says she has a remedy for such and such. On the next one, you'll see a shamanic healer who says he has seen the equivalent of autism happen in many guises throughout his many past lives. You'll get all of it.

What do you do with all this conflicting information? You take it back inside. It's not what you think about these approaches. It's about how they feel to you. Is one intriguing to you? Does it make you curious? Can you feel it in your body? Even if your child is nonverbal, you can say, "Here's what we are going to try next." Often, just by telling them what you're going to try next, their behaviors start to change immediately because they get the vibration of the situation even before the event has arrived. If a particular approach doesn't feel right, skip it and go on to the next thing.

If you're spending more time in the moment, you always know what's good for you in the moment, and you always know what's not good for you in the moment. Before long, you'll be able to read nuances of feeling, both your own and your child's. Each week try something that you may feel a bit uncomfortable about. First watch it on YouTube, and if it feels right, give it a try. You don't have to tell your mother or your husband or anyone else that you're watching something that you "shouldn't" be watching. I would highly advise that you not tell any skeptics about the new technique that you're trying or anything else that's new. Wait and see what works, and let them ask you what has changed. In the meantime, talk to those who can support you. You will be surprised, as you begin to explore and open up, just how many people who are out there trying the same thing. You'll begin attracting therapists, physicians, and all kinds of support from those that you may have thought would not be open. That is true no matter what you try, because like energy will always attract like energy. We feel so ingrained with the idea that we're not allowed to step out of the model that we're in. But you can. If I can do anything for you, it's to give you permission to explore past the boundaries that society typically sets.

To sum up: What do you do next? Find new approaches that represent the kind of outside-the-box thinking that feels right to you. And keep on trying them. They are a lot less likely to cause harm to your child than putting her on yet another new drug. You can't mess up a child's biochemistry through herbal treatments, through massage, through kinesiology, or through pretty much any of the alternative treatments that are available today, and there are plenty of alternative professionals out there that you will feel comfortable with. So, as you can see, there is little if any downside in trying something new.

But more important than what you do is how you are. Set the vibrational tone. Be in touch with yourself. Be in the now. Become the sensor and reader of what works for your child. Become the bridge between the level of physical and mental functioning and the level of soul/spirit experience. Let being trump doing, and suddenly you'll find yourself more at peace with yourself than ever before, more at peace with the fact that your child possesses this diagnosis, and more at peace with your child. And isn't that what you were after all along? In the long run we aren't trying to "fix" anything, only becoming more comfortable with what is. We are simply weaning off of all the "shoulds" and "shouldn'ts" so we allow the Awesomism to emerge.

Chapter 10

A Vision of the Future

In the short term, if you apply some of the ideas that we've discussed in this book, you'll end up with a deeper relationship and connection with your children—not just those diagnosed with autism, but all of your children. The behaviors associated with autism will diminish as a result of the approaches we have discussed. Interaction within your family—between you and your spouse, between parents and all the children, will get easier all the way around. So the first thing that will happen is that your home will be a more peaceful, relaxed, happy place for all of you. Most importantly, you will feel more empowerment to make great decisions for your children. You will know your children at all levels of their being, and you will feel much more comfortable knowing that they will show you or reflect back to you just what is needed.

But it doesn't stop there. Then we get to step out just a little bit more, because you're going to be able to provide a model of this different approach to the diagnosis of autism—and to the challenge of raising all children—for other people. You'll actually be able to educate people who don't have this awareness. So now you'll be educating doctors, teachers, and therapists about your model as well. This will broaden the horizon of the child all the way around, because you'll be helping to raise the vibration of all of the individuals with whom your child comes into meaningful contact. In so doing, your child will feel more comfortable being who she is, so that she can bring all of her gifts to the planet. You start off by creating that environment in the home. Next, you start to create that bit by bit in your child's school. Other parents are also doing the same thing, so you won't be the only one.

As a result, schools will change to accommodate the needs of your child—the true needs of your child. Doctors will start to change to accommodate the needs of your child and the true needs of all children diagnosed with autism. And now we'll establish a vibration that is a consciousness that allows these children to fully bring themselves front and center. And when they do that, we get to see for the first time what it is truly like to function as a high-vibrational being. We get to see the intuitive skills of these children. We truly get to see their ability to communicate beyond time and space. We get to see their ability to heal and their ability to know what is right for the moment, not only for themselves but maybe, in a broader perspective, for all of us. And as we start making these alterations in our own approach, then the energy of the whole thing just keeps on building to a point where we will be in an environment where all of us function more from a spirit or soul base instead of a mental base or a physical base. And when that happens, we'll have a whole population of people who understand that they're in this world but not of it, just as these children are already.

Children diagnosed with autism are in this world but not of it. As Riley communicated to me, "Children diagnosed with autism are stuck between two worlds." That's why they look so funny or different to us in the first place. It won't be that way forever. As the vibration of our humanity rises, so does the ability of these children to more profoundly and concretely offer their awareness to the world. They currently offer that gift simply by being here. The vibration that they embody is gift enough, and the training that they offer their caregivers is bringing greater and greater awareness all the time to what actually lies hidden inside. In many ways we are becoming more like them as we attempt to have them become more like us. We are already starting to rise to the occasion. Our first baby steps are to have a whole humanity that has the potential to function from a place of "Does this feel like it's what we want to do?" instead of "This is the way things have to be done." The potential to come to a balance between the left and right brain function is so strong in this situation. One in 150 families are now being "trained" in moving from left-hemisphere dominance into more right-hemisphere function, from a sense of separation to the awareness of oneness, from a sense of relating to their life experience as only physical and mental reality to being with the pure soul emotion and vibration that links us all. The whole thing will be global and beyond.

We'll be asking and answering new questions about ourselves. Are we living and being the way we truly want to be? What changes will happen as a result of that? And these children are here to show us this, every step of the way. Up until now, humanity has been missing the mark. We haven't had the model that these children are providing for us. But as soon as we understand that model, it will be like a very small seed that we've planted now has potential to transform the world. The whole oak tree is in an acorn, and the future of the world is in the spirit of these children. It's all there. That magnificence is all there. And it will just keep growing and getting bigger and transforming consciousness until our whole world is transformed.

The result will be a world in which every human being operates, like the true spiritual masters they are, instead of a humanity that is functioning out of fear. The potential of this transformation is unlimited. It just keeps going and growing and, and it's going to get nicer. It's going to be more comfortable to be in the challenging position in which you find yourself as a parent of a child diagnosed with autism. Getting comfortable with these kids is the first step, in my opinion, in a spiritual transformation that will leave no corner of the world untouched. Within a short period of time, we will have a humanity that functions more from a place and spirit than what we have now. And if that happens, we'll be in really good hands. That's why every time I see one of these children, I know I'm looking at Awesomism. We will be in really good hands, if we simply understand what is in front of us. Why would we want to drag them down from their lofty spiritual perch when you consider the potential of what they're here to teach us? That's why we have to move out of our comfort zone in terms of treating them. It's not until we do so that we'll actually see what's right in front of us. It's always been there, but it was never available to us until now.

We need to look at our children diagnosed with autism with a new pair of glasses. Not rose-colored glasses, in which we pretend that everything's easy and everything's all right. Because if you are the parent of a child diagnosed with autism, there is a new experience ahead, in fact a new reality.. Yes, as we've discussed, it can seem as if you do have more of a burden than the parent whose child does not have this diagnosis. There's no question about that, and I do not want anything in this book to be misconstrued so that you might think I'm saying, "It's all easy," or "You've got nothing to be concerned about." You are handling a lot, probably more than you ever realized, and my heart goes out to you as you continue to display the bravery and courage that it takes to help your child be the fullest expression of himself that he can be, especially within a culture that has such a low tolerance for difference.

But I'm just asking you to pull the camera back and take in the broader picture. These children are here for a reason. The lessons they are here to teach us are happening now for a reason. An old expression says, when the student is ready, the teacher appears. We are not just caregivers or caretakers of these children—we are their students. We have so much to learn from them, as individuals, as families, as societies, as a collective humanity. Let's replace our fear and distress with love and faith, because as we connect with our children diagnosed with autism and see just how awesome they are, they are going to lead us to a place more awesome than any of us could ever have imagined. I wish the best for you and your child on your journey, and if there's anything else I can do for you, I'm here to help.

That was no average experience with Riley back in 1999. If his gift to me could create this … just imagine what your own relationship with your child can create. Awesomism! It's all just beginning!

3234165

Made in the USA